by Rand Hummel

BJU PRESS
GREENVILLE, SOUTH CAROLINA

This textbook was written by members of the faculty and staff of Bob Jones University. Standing for the "old-time religion" and the absolute authority of the Bible since 1927, Bob Jones University is the world's leading Fundamentalist Christian university. The staff of the University is devoted to educating Christian men and women to be servants of Jesus Christ in all walks of life.

Providing unparalleled academic excellence, Bob Jones University prepares its students through its offering of over 120 majors, while its fervent spiritual emphasis prepares their minds and hearts for service and devotion to the Lord Jesus Christ.

If you would like more information about the spiritual and academic opportunities available at Bob Jones University, please call
1-800-BJ-AND-ME (1-800-252-6363).
www.bju.edu

NOTE:

The fact that materials produced by other publishers may be referred to in this volume does not constitute an endorsement by BJU Press of the content or theological position of materials produced by such publishers. The position of BJU Press, and of Bob Jones University, is well known. Any references and ancillary materials are listed as an aid to the student or the teacher and in an attempt to maintain the accepted academic standards of the publishing industry.

All Scripture is quoted from the Authorized King James Version.

The Dark Side of the Internet

Writers:
Text by Rand Hummel
Essays by Michael Osborne, MA,
and Thomas Parr, MA
Editors: Elizabeth Bang Berg
with Michael Osborne
and Thomas Parr
Biblical Integration: Bryan Smith, PhD
and Will Gray, MA
Project Manager: Dan Woodhull

Designer: John Bjerk
Cover Designers: Elly Kalagayan and
David Siglin
Illustrators: Cory Godbey,
Julie Arsenault,
and Annie Bastine
Compositors: Jennifer Hearing
and Beata Augustyniak
Photo Acquisition: Carla Thomas

The following agencies and individuals have furnished materials to meet the photographic needs of this textbook. We wish to express our gratitude to them for their important contribution.
Cover: Unusual Films
Chapter 6: COREL Corporation 54

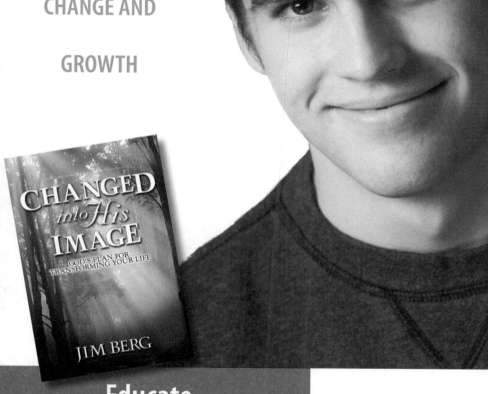

Contents

INTRODUCTION

"Hey Rand, can I talk to you?"

"Sure, what's up?"

"I don't think I can talk without crying, but I'll try. The other night, about two in the morning, something woke me up. I walked down the hall and looked into the living room—and there was my dad, looking at pornography on the computer. I don't know what to do. Do I tell my mom? I don't think I can talk to my dad. Can you help me, please?"

Conversations such as the one above are increasingly more common and more heartbreaking every day. With the advent of the Internet, there are not only incredible research opportunities and high-speed communication possibilities but also the constant availability of sin. For years, Satan has been hurling fiery darts at young believers. Today, he's gotten his hands on a high-powered rifle—the Dark Side of the Internet.

The Internet has opened doors of communication with missionaries and fellow believers worldwide. There is a lot of good that can come from this technology. Our concern is not the technology but that evil men, controlled by an evil master, are using the Internet to tempt and trap many of God's people into sinning, thus destroying their relationship with family members, friends, and God. My prayer is that the Bible principles in this study will be effective in helping guard God's people from becoming caught in the Dark Side of the Internet.

A Fast-Changing and Dangerous World

We live in a fast-changing world. You can hardly go through a day, or even an hour, without hearing the phrase *dot-com*. The Internet is part of our lives and is not going to go away. It's going to get bigger and stronger and faster and more appealing every single day. You see, the Internet of today is much like the invention of the telephone over a hundred years ago. Below is a Western Union memo dating back to 1876 (the year you teens think your parents started high school). This memo is commenting on the brand new invention of a communication device known as the *telephone*.[1]

> This telephone has too many shortcomings to be
> seriously considered as a means of communication.
> The device is inherently of no value to us.

Can you imagine what it would be like to live without a telephone today? We are controlled not only by telephones, but also by cell phones, beepers, pagers, PDAs, and a whole barrage of communication toys.

With the growing expansion of the Internet affecting many areas of our lives, there will be even more opportunities to search the web, chat with friends, go shopping, and create webpages—all with the possibilities of speeds hundreds of times faster than today's Internet connections.

In our high-tech society, the computers we use today will probably become antiques within the next ten years. For instance, in your home, your refrigerator, your toaster, your DVD player—everything will become computerized! You could be on your way to work when your cell phone rings and it's your refrigerator calling you. Your new and improved refrigerator will have the technology to know everything that it has inside. Somehow, every time you put something inside it, it scans the food and records it on a list. So, your fridge calls you and says, "While you're on your way home from work, would you mind stopping at the grocery store and picking up a gallon of milk; oh, and while you're at it, how about two or three dozen Krispy Kreme donuts!" Or maybe you will be driving down the road and your PDA buzzes you—it's your DVD recorder calling! It knows your

incredible love for, let's say, *Winnie the Pooh and Tigger Too* and knows there is a twenty-four hour marathon on TV and wants to know if you want it to record it for you. We live in a high-tech society, and this technology is going to get only more advanced as time goes on.

The Internet of today is a technological marvel. But there is a Dark Side of the Internet that is pervasive and sometimes hard to avoid. The Internet is a new type of danger for all of us.

I did not realize it was such a grave danger until a few years ago while preaching in a Christian school. It was one of those Christian schools where most of the senior high students had absolutely no heart for God. Many just sat back and rolled their eyes during the preaching. One of the boys got right with the Lord and shared with me the source of such hardened hearts. As he put it, "A lot of the guys in my school go home at night and surf the web to find the most wicked, perverse, disgusting sites you can imagine. The next day they share those addresses with each other and go home that night to watch the trash and laugh about it with each other."

In another incident, a group of girls were heavily involved in Internet chatrooms. Some of the girls met a guy named Luke and, for whatever reason, Luke chose to chat with just two or three of the girls and none of the others. So the girls Luke wouldn't chat with got upset with those girls who were chatting and started a hate movement, which resulted in incredible disunity.[2]

With a burdened heart, I began digging into God's Word to find passages that could help me as I counsel those who have been involved with the misuse of this technology—a misuse that is destroying so many hearts and homes. I came across a description of a vision God gave His young prophet Ezekiel. Ezekiel's vision, in a way, is being repeated in churches, schools, homes, and youth groups today. What God told Ezekiel many years ago, we need to hear today.

This study will be neither highly technical nor cover every aspect of the Internet. It is a simple approach for each one of us who may not be computer geeks or even computer literate to learn how to avoid the Dark Side of the Internet.

---

[1]Linda Stone, "Virtually Yours: The Internet as a Social Medium," VISION, April 14, 1997, http://www.research.microsoft.com/vwg/papers/VISION.html.

[2]Please note that names and details of illustrations in this book have been changed to protect the identities of individuals.

EZEKIEL'S VISION

1

God's Word is packed full of principles that can easily be applied to modern-day issues but sometimes are not so easy to find. A trip to *Strong's Concordance* looking for words such as Internet, computer, website, chatrooms, television, or media will not provide much help. Are there any passages in the Bible that could apply to the misuse of the Internet? During my study I came across a verse in Ezekiel 8 concerning God's vision to Ezekiel that refers to *sinning in the dark*. I was amazed how the vision teaches principles that could and should govern Internet access today. What was happening in Ezekiel's day is happening today! I know that God did not give Ezekiel his vision to deal solely with the Dark Side of the Internet, but what God showed Ezekiel hundreds of years ago is going on in the midst of God's people today.

Ezekiel was not an elderly, white-bearded prophet but was actually only twenty-five years of age when taken into captivity and around thirty when called into the prophetic ministry. He was a prophet about the same time that Jeremiah, who was about twenty years older, and Daniel, who was around the same age as Ezekiel, ministered to God's people. Ezekiel and his wife were among the thousands of Jews taken captive to Babylon around 597 BC (2 Kings 24:11–18). Heartbroken Ezekiel wrote of his wife's death (Ezekiel 24:18). The book of Ezekiel does not mention Ezekiel's death, but tradition suggests it occurred thirty years after the death of his wife at the hands of an Israelite prince whose idolatry he had rebuked.

The book of Ezekiel is saturated with the teachings of the glory of God, the holiness of God, and the sovereignty of God. The *glory of the Lord* seems to be a central theme in Ezekiel, appearing in chapters 1, 3, 10, 11, 43, and 44. God's holiness, power, and glory are often magnified as they are painted on the backdrop of Judah's sin (Ezekiel 1:26–28; 43:1–7).

God's Jealousy

Let's sit back and concentrate as we slowly walk through Ezekiel's vision and see how it applies to so many of God's people today and to their interaction with the Dark Side of the Internet.

> And it came to pass in the sixth year, in the sixth month, in the fifth day of the month, as I sat in mine house, and the elders of Judah sat before me, that the hand of the Lord God fell there upon me. Then I beheld, and lo a likeness as the appearance of fire: from the appearance of his loins even downward, fire; and from his loins even upward, as the appearance of brightness, as the colour of amber. And he put forth the form of an hand, and took me by a lock of mine head; and the spirit lifted me up between the earth and the heaven, and brought me in the visions of God to Jerusalem, to the door of the inner gate that looketh toward the north; where was the seat of the image of jealousy, which provoketh to jealousy. And, behold, the glory of the God of Israel was there, according to the vision that I saw in the plain. Then said he unto me, Son of man, lift up thine eyes now the way toward the north. So I lifted up mine eyes the way toward the north, and behold northward at the gate of the altar *this image of jealousy in the entry.* (Ezekiel 8:1–5)

"Image of jealousy" refers to an idol the Jews had set up in the temple that provoked God to jealousy.

Now, when the Bible speaks of God's jealousy, it is different from the jealousy that people often experience. Man's jealousy is focused on man— his pleasure and happiness. God's jealousy is focused on God—His honor and glory. God is the greatest, most valuable being there is, and none can compare to Him (1 Samuel 2:2). Therefore, He is rightly jealous for our total devotion to Him. But this jealousy also has man's best interests at heart since man's greatest good is loving and serving God. God wants our love for Him to be shared with no other god. God is jealous *for* us. God knows that if we love the world with its eye-pleasing, flesh-satisfying, prideful temptations, we cannot and will not love Him as we should.

> Love not the world, neither the things that are in the world. If any man love the world, the love of the Father is not in him. For all that is in the world, the lust of the flesh, and the lust of the eyes, and the pride of life, is not of the Father, but is of the world. And the world passeth away, and the lust thereof: but he that doeth the will of God abideth for ever. (1 John 2:15–17)

The bottom line is that God wants the best for your life. God does not want you to fall in love with anything that will pull your heart away from Him and ruin your life! He does not want you to make decisions that just a few months from now will torment you. God loves you so much, He does not want the pull of the world to pull you to pieces. God is a jealous God! He loves you and wants what is best for you. For this reason, please listen to Him. Take a few minutes and think about the following verses and what they say about God:

> There is none holy as the Lord: for there is none beside thee: neither is there any rock like our God.
> 1 Samuel 2:2

> Thou shalt not make unto thee any graven image, or any likeness of any thing that is in heaven above, or that is in the earth beneath, or that is in the water under the earth: Thou shalt not bow down thyself to them, nor serve them: for I the Lord thy God am a jealous God, visiting the iniquity of the fathers upon the children unto the third and fourth generation of them that hate me; And shewing mercy unto thousands of them that love me, and keep my commandments. (Exodus 20:4–6)

> Take heed unto yourselves, lest ye forget the covenant of the Lord your God, which he made with you, and make you a graven image, or the likeness of any thing, which the Lord thy God hath forbidden thee. For the Lord thy God is a consuming fire, even a jealous God. (Deuteronomy 4:23–24)

3

Forsaking Abominations, Drawing Near to God

> He said furthermore unto me, Son of man, seest thou
> what they do? even the great *abominations* that the
> house of Israel committeth here, that I should go far
> off from my sanctuary? but turn thee yet again, and
> thou shalt see *greater abominations*. (Ezekiel 8:6)

Whenever you read the word *abomination*, you should think "hate, hate, hate." If you want to know exactly what God hates, get *Strong's Concordance* and read every verse in the Bible that has the word *abomination* in it. Make a list of what is abominable to God and then ask God to give you the same hatred for those things that God hates.

God said, "Ezekiel, do you see what my people are doing? They are literally driving me out of their lives by choosing the very abominations that I hate!" God wants to be close to us—but we often distance ourselves from Him so we can enjoy sin. Here is a great, life-changing Bible truth that is taught throughout Scripture but is clearly expressed in James 4:8:

> Draw nigh to God, and he will draw nigh to you. Cleanse
> your hands, ye sinners; and purify your hearts, ye double
> minded.

We can be as close to God as we want to be!

If we keep our hands cleansed by getting rid of everything in life that makes it "easy" to sin and keep our hearts purified by immediate confession of sin, then we can draw near to God. Our dirty hands and defiled hearts drive us away from close fellowship with God. What is in your room at home? What is hidden in your basement or garage that feeds a filthy heart? What relationship at school or church so consumes your heart and mind that it is all you think about? Can you think of anything in your life that needs to be "cleansed" or "purified"? If so, set this book down, find a quiet place, and get on your knees before our loving, holy God. Draw near to God through confession of sin and praise Him for His incredible, undeserved forgiveness. He promises that if we draw near to Him, He will draw near to us. Before we go on in the Ezekiel passage, meditate on this song, which helps us remember the joy and responsibility of being near to our great Lord.

By *Cleland B. McAfee*

There is a place of quiet rest,
Near to the heart of God,
A place where sin cannot molest,
Near to the heart of God.

There is a place of comfort sweet,
Near to the heart of God,
A place where we our Savior meet,
Near to the heart of God.

There is a place of full release,
Near to the heart of God,
A place where all is joy and peace,
Near to the heart of God.

O Jesus, blest Redeemer,
Sent from the heart of God,
Hold us, who wait before Thee,
Near to the heart of God.

Idolatry, Old and New

And he brought me to the door of the court; and when I looked, behold a hole in the wall. Then said he unto me, Son of man, dig now in the wall: and when I had digged in the wall, behold a door. And he said unto me, Go in, and behold the wicked abominations that they do here. *So I went in and saw; and behold every form of creeping things, and abominable beasts, and all the idols of the house of Israel, pourtrayed upon the wall round about.* (Ezekiel 8:7–10)

When Ezekiel dug through the wall and found the door, he walked in and saw the wicked graffiti of the most perverse, filthy abominations imaginable. On the walls of this sinful hideout, the wickedness of God's people (specifically, God's spiritual leaders) was portrayed. Careful study reveals that many of the rites, incantations, practices, and activities associated with the idolatrous worship of that day were often lewd, disgusting, revolting, and nauseating. Pictured on the walls were perverse depictions of filthiness, immorality, and violence.

5

A simple click of a mouse on many websites can bring you face to face with the same kind of wickedness. Every type of perverse, wicked immorality can be found portrayed "upon the wall" of the Dark Side of the Internet.

God's People Involved

> And there stood before them seventy *men of the ancients* of the house of Israel, and in the midst of them stood Jaazaniah the son of Shaphan, with every man his censer in his hand; and a thick cloud of incense went up. (Ezekiel 8:11)

The Dark Side of the Internet is not a problem just for teens. Even in conservative, Christian circles moms are leaving their kids and husbands because they have found what they think is their "true love" in chatrooms on the Internet. Dads are daily becoming addicted to the evil, drug-like pornography that is openly displayed on the walls of the Dark Side of the Internet. It is unbelievable. It is heartbreaking!

Covetousness . . . is idolatry.

Who is Jaazaniah? Jaazaniah was the son of Shaphan, the scribe who read the Word of God to King Josiah. King Josiah was truly broken when he heard how God's people were in such rebellion and sin (see 2 Kings 22:3–13).

Jaazaniah heard his father read the Word of God. Those of you reading this book are probably much like Jaazaniah and have heard the Word of God read and preached throughout most of your life. Many of you come from Christian families. You know the truth. You have been taught what God loves and what God hates. For those of you who have repented of your sins and asked God for His forgiveness and saving grace, you are considered God's people.

In this passage God is saying, "Do you see what's going on in the midst of *my* people?"—not those who don't believe in God but those who profess to know God.

"Private" Sinning

> Then said he unto me, Son of man, hast thou seen what the ancients of the house of Israel do *in the dark*, every man in the chamber of his imagery? for they say, *The Lord seeth us not*; the Lord hath forsaken the earth. (Ezekiel 8:12)

There is a false sense of privacy involved in the Dark Side of the Internet. This verse speaks of what the ancients, the supposedly spiritual leaders of the day, did when they thought no one was watching, not even God. They sought to cover their wickedness by hiding in the dark. Today, it is too easy to hide your sin. All you have to do is to walk into your bedroom, shut your door, and turn on your computer. Do you ever think, "No one will ever find out. No one will ever know"? Many foolishly believe that the Lord does not notice what is going on or does not really care.

Greater Abominations

> He said also unto me, Turn thee yet again, and thou shalt see *greater abominations* that they do. (Ezekiel 8:13)

What could be worse?

> Then he brought me to the door of the gate of the Lord's house which was toward the north; and, behold, there sat women weeping for Tammuz. (Ezekiel 8:14)

Tammuz was originally a Babylonian sun-god, called Dumuzu or Duzu, the husband of Ishtar, who corresponds to Aphrodite of the Greeks. The Babylonian myth represents Tammuz as a beautiful shepherd slain by a wild boar. Ishtar mourned a long time for him. This mourning for Tammuz was celebrated in Babylon by women on the second day of the fourth month, which thus became known as Tammuz. The cult rites involved in this worship were incredibly wicked, including perverted, gross immorality.

> Then said he unto me, Hast thou seen this, O son of man? turn thee yet again, and thou shalt see *greater abominations* than these. (Ezekiel 8:15)

This is the third time the Lord used a similar phrase in this passage.

> . . . but turn thee yet again, and thou shalt see *greater abominations*. (Ezekiel 8:6)

> . . . Turn thee yet again, and thou shalt see *greater abominations* that they do. (Ezekiel 8:13)

One of the dangers of the Dark Side of the Internet is that there is no end to the wickedness. Books have final chapters, movies have a time limit, and music has a conclusion. However, there is no end to the Dark Side of the Internet—it goes on and on and on—getting more disgusting and more deviant the deeper you dig.

The sins involved with the Dark Side of the Internet can be very addicting and desensitizing. What was once exciting becomes boring. What at one time made you blush at its wickedness doesn't even faze you anymore. What you once hated you now look for.

Growing up, I had the privilege of working on a number of farms. It was not too hard to find work baling hay or cleaning cow stalls. I remember working in the barn and someone would walk in, comment on  how bad it smelled, and ask me how I could stand the terrible smell. I would usually answer, "What smell? I don't smell anything!" Sometimes I would run to the house and ask my grandma for a glass of iced tea, and she would stop me at the door: "Wait outside—you're not coming in the house stinking like that!" I thought, stinking like what? I don't smell anything. You know, when you work in that stuff every day, the smell begins to permeate your hair, your skin, and your clothes. After a while, it just doesn't stink anymore. If you through music, television, and the Dark Side of the Internet allow sensuality to permeate your mind and heart, you will find that sin just doesn't stink anymore.

Leadership at Risk

> And he brought me into the inner court of the Lord's
> house, and, behold, at the door of the temple of the
> Lord, between the porch and the altar, were about *five
> and twenty men*, with their backs toward the temple of
> the Lord, and their faces toward the east; *and they wor-
> shipped the sun* toward the east. (Ezekiel 8:16)

God brought Ezekiel into the inner court of the temple. Ezekiel
saw twenty-five men who turned their backs on God's temple and
began worshiping God's creation rather than the Creator Himself.
These twenty-five men represented spiritual leaders in Israel. God
was showing Ezekiel that even those in high leadership positions had
chosen to turn their backs on God.

Sin: No Big Deal?

> Then he said unto me, Hast thou seen this, O son of
> man? *Is it a light thing* to the house of Judah that they
> commit the abominations which they commit here? for
> they have filled the land with violence, and have re-
> turned to provoke me to anger: and, lo, they put the
> branch to their nose. (Ezekiel 8:17)

In this verse, God asks Ezekiel a very convicting question:

> *Is it a light thing* to the house of Judah that they com-
> mit the abominations which they commit here?

Today, we would ask the question one of these ways. Is it nothing
to these people that they commit these terrible sins? Is it no big deal?
Doesn't it bother God's people that they are choosing to love that
which God hates? Is there no conviction in the hearts of professing
believers who are living in such sin? Is it a light thing? Doesn't it
bother *you*? Doesn't it rip your heart out when you choose to sin right
in the face of God? Don't you care anymore?

Actually, this is a great question for us to ask ourselves. If we can sin
and it not bother us, there is something wrong in our hearts. Conviction
of heart is a great indicator that the Spirit of God lives within. Conviction reminds us that we are God's children and He will constantly
remind us to stay in His will. Conviction is like a whistle-blowing ref-
eree when we step out-of-bounds. Psalm 37:23 says, "The steps of a
good man are ordered by the Lord." The word *order* does not refer to
an army colonel giving his men their orders but to a loving Lord who
sets each step of our lives in a preordained path. When we step off that

path and start to get entangled with the thorns and briars of this world, God lets us know through conviction. When was the last time you sensed God's conviction in your heart? Meditate on the following verses and ask God to reveal to you if you are living like those in Ezekiel's day who thought it was "no big deal" to sin against God.

This then is the message which we have heard of him, and declare unto you, that God is light, and in him is no darkness at all. If we say that we have fellowship with him, and walk in darkness, we lie, and do not the truth: But if we walk in the light, as he is in the light, we have fellowship one with another, and the blood of Jesus Christ his Son cleanseth us from all sin. If we say that we have no sin, we deceive ourselves, and the truth is not in us. If we confess our sins, he is faithful and just to forgive us our sins, and to cleanse us from all unrighteousness. If we say that we have not sinned, we make him a liar, and his word is not in us. (1 John 1:5–10)

If you find that you don't really care about these truths from God's Word, your unconcern may be a sign that you are not God's child (1 Corinthians 16:22). You need to pray that God will grant you "repentance to the acknowledging of the truth" (2 Timothy 2:25). You are a rebel, condemned to an eternity of anguish and torment (Romans 3:23; 6:23; Revelation 21:8). But Christ died in the place of sinners such as you (1 Timothy 1:15). He saves from God's just wrath everyone who trusts Him as Savior from sin (John 3:16; Romans 5:9–10). But a glib prayer does not save anyone. Only people who realize that

they are sinners and cry out to God with that understanding will receive the salvation Christ offers (Luke 18:10–14). If you've never felt remorse over your sin and still don't, your first prayer ought to be, "Lord, make me hate my sin and love Jesus Christ."

The Sin of Violence

For they have filled the land with *violence.* . . .

We will look more closely at the violence issue later. The violent mindset and total disregard for life that can be seen in many of the computer-based games and terrorist-based websites is unbelievable. God hates violence! One of the reasons the world was destroyed with the Flood was that the earth was filled with violence.

And God said unto Noah, The end of all flesh is come before me; for the earth is filled with violence through them; and, behold, I will destroy them with the earth. (Genesis 6:13)

Provoking God

. . . and have returned *to provoke me to anger.*

When you truly love someone, you do all you can to keep from making him or her angry. Do you love God? Are there times in your life that you choose to provoke God to anger? We must constantly remind ourselves to refuse to be a part of anything that provokes God to anger. Note the following verses:

But fornication, and all uncleanness, or covetousness, let it not be once named among you, as becometh saints; Neither filthiness, nor foolish talking, nor jesting, which are not convenient: but rather giving of thanks. For this ye know, that no whoremonger, nor unclean person, nor covetous man, who is an idolater, hath any inheritance in the kingdom of Christ and of God. Let no man deceive you with vain words: for because of these things cometh the wrath of God upon the children of disobedience. Be not ye therefore partakers with them. (Ephesians 5:3–7)

Mortify therefore your members which are upon the earth; fornication, uncleanness, inordinate affection, evil concupiscence, and covetousness, which is idolatry: For which things' sake the wrath of God cometh on the children of disobedience. (Colossians 3:5–6)

Ezekiel finishes verse 17 with this phrase:

> . . . and, lo, they put the branch to their nose.

This is not an easy phrase to interpret, but it was probably some sort of idolatrous religious ritual that blasphemed God.

God's Response to Sin

The last verse of Ezekiel's vision is a very sad verse. God promises to punish those who love what He hates and hate what He loves.

> Therefore will I also deal in fury: mine eye shall not spare, neither will I have pity: and though they cry in mine ears with a loud voice, yet will I not hear them. (Ezekiel 8:18)

What does this verse mean? Is it saying that God will not forgive us when we sin? No! Is there no hope to those who through curiosity have peeked at the Dark Side of the Internet? We must remember that this verse was given to Israelites in Ezekiel's day who had completely apostatized from God. His message to them was that He was planning to punish them, and nothing could change that plan. This message is still the same for apostates today. Now I would like to discuss three general principles taught in this verse.

Get the Big Picture

1. God is *jealous*!
2. God is *holy* and will not overlook sin.
3. God is *just,* and even though we can choose our sin, we cannot choose the consequences of our sin.

God is jealous!

God loves us so much and knows us so well that He constantly reminds us to stay away from sin. He knows what wicked and sinful affections will draw our hearts away from Him. He will deal in fury and wrath with those who choose such sin. God's anger is never expressed in a wrong way, but it is expressed, since God hates sin and sin makes Him angry. Meditate on these passages that describe God's anger against sin:

And when the people complained, it displeased the Lord: and the Lord heard it; and his anger was kindled; and the fire of the Lord burnt among them, and consumed them that were in the uttermost parts of the camp. (Numbers 11:1)

Ye shall not go after other gods, of the gods of the people which are round about you; (For the Lord thy God is a jealous God among you) lest the anger of the Lord thy God be kindled against thee, and destroy thee from off the face of the earth. (Deuteronomy 6:14–15)

The Lord is merciful and gracious, slow to anger, and plenteous in mercy. He will not always chide: neither will he keep his anger for ever. He hath not dealt with us after our sins; nor rewarded us according to our iniquities. For as the heaven is high above the earth, so great is his mercy toward them that fear him. (Psalm 103:8–11)

God is holy and will not overlook sin.
Too many Christians today think that God is like a permissive dad or mom who overlooks our sin and selfishness, hoping that they will just go away. God will not overlook those who choose to oppose His Word. We are reminded of this many times in the Bible.

Yet they say, The Lord shall not see, neither shall the God of Jacob regard it. Understand, ye brutish among the people: and ye fools, when will ye be wise? He that planted the ear, shall he not hear? he that formed the eye, shall he not see? (Psalm 94:7–9)

For the ways of man are before the eyes of the Lord, and he pondereth all his goings. (Proverbs 5:21)

The eyes of the Lord are in every place, beholding the evil and the good. (Proverbs 15:3)

God is just, and even though we can choose our sin, we cannot choose the consequences of our sin.
God's people were already suffering from the consequences of their sin. They chose to love what God hated and drove God out of their lives. When God's enemies attacked His people, they ripped them away from their homeland, put them in bondage, and turned free men into slaves. Men and boys were used and treated like animals while many of the women and girls were treated even worse. In other words,

the bondage and slavery that God's people suffered was simply the consequence of their own sin. We can choose our sin, but we cannot choose the consequences of our sin. God does forgive, but He does not always remove the consequences. Those who get caught in immorality may regain their relationship with God, but they never regain their former relationship with their family. Proverbs 6:33 says, "A wound and dishonour shall he get; and his reproach shall not be wiped away."

It is amazing how selfish and self-centered we can be. We cry out to God when life is hard and pressures are great; but as soon as things are "back to normal," we forget God and live our selfish lives again. It is a terrible cycle to be caught in. We see this same cycle in the book of Judges. God's people would live to please self until things got hard and the consequences were too tough to handle, and then they would cry out to God for deliverance. God would send a judge (for example, Gideon, Samson, or Shamgar) to deliver His people from bondage. Once they were free, it was no time at all until they walked back into the same sin that caused the judgment in the first place. It is amazing to see how many Christians today sin on Monday, ask for forgiveness Monday night to relieve the pressure of conviction, and go right back to the same sin on Tuesday. Remember, God will forgive, but He may not remove the consequences that could dog you for the rest of your life.

ITS POWER

2

And there stood before them seventy men of the ancients of the house of Israel, and in the midst of them
stood Jaazaniah the son of Shaphan, with every man
his censer in his hand; and a thick cloud of incense
went up. (Ezekiel 8:11)

No One Is Beyond Its Power

There is no one beyond the power and the pull of the Dark Side of
the Internet—no one. No matter how godly, how influential, how
popular, or how old—no one. Not your parents, not your pastor, not
your youth leaders, not your counselor, not your best friend, not even
you. No one is beyond the power and the pull of the Dark Side of the
Internet. Statistics are constantly changing, and the number of men
choosing to be involved in Internet pornography is growing on a daily
basis. In 1998 there were an estimated 14 million pornographic webpages compared to the 260 million in 2003.[1] Pastors are losing their
ministries, families are breaking up, the minds of little children are
being polluted, and teens by the boatloads are turning their backs on
God. This is spiritual warfare!

Bible Examples and Instruction

Who was one of the strongest men in the Bible? Samson. What
destroyed his spiritual life and testimony? It was his incredible lust
or desire for strange
women. Who was
one of the wisest
kings in the Bible?
Solomon. He had
three hundred wives
and seven hundred
concubines. These
strange women
turned his heart away
from God. Who was
one of the godliest

kings in all the Bible? David. How old was David when he committed adultery with Bathsheba? He was around fifty! His boys were already in their mid-twenties. Did David love God? Yes! Did David meditate on God's Word? Yes! Did David sit and write psalms of praise to God? Yes! Did David have a heart for God? Yes! Did David sin? Yes!

We must constantly remind ourselves that there is no one beyond the power and the pull of the Dark Side of the Internet. The Bible warns us that we are all capable of committing any sin.

> Wherefore let him that thinketh he standeth take heed [watch out, be careful] lest he fall. (1 Corinthians 10:12)

> Watch and pray, that ye enter not into temptation: the spirit indeed is willing, but the flesh is weak. (Matthew 26:41)

> For she [the strange woman] hath cast down many wounded: yea [Get this], many strong men have been slain by her. (Proverbs 7:26)

Focus on the Family has a pastoral care line reserved just for pastors. One out of seven calls are from pastors begging for help because of their struggle with Internet pornography.[2]

Online Relationships

Is it just the men that Satan is targeting, or does the Internet offer a problem for women? While men are often drawn by visual temptation, women often seek "meaningful" relationships: someone who cares and has enough time to listen, to talk, to communicate. Inappropriate electronic relationships are a great problem. You see, these online "chats" and communications begin very innocently, or at the most flirtatiously. Electronic relationships are distorted and very dangerous. Why? You don't know who you're talking to!

You don't know who you're talking to!

Talking online is very deceiving. It seems safe to type on a keyboard and hide behind a computer screen. Even people who are very shy all of a sudden become very bold in what they say and the type of conversations they enter. Most forget that they don't know who they're talking to!

Consider the example of a case where an FBI agent, posing as a teenaged girl, signed on a "youth" chatroom. Of the twenty-two other "youths," all twenty-two of them ended up being adults wanting to entrap girls.[3] There is a dark world of perverted individuals who stalk teens and children on the Internet to befriend, to chat with, to build an online relationship with, to get a real address for, and finally to get what is called a "face to face." These wicked people have one goal in mind—to someday meet and abuse.

God's Power Is Greater

Sound scary? Good, it should. The Devil and his cronies are not to be trifled with. But Christians can rejoice that "greater is he that is in you, than he that is in the world" (1 John 4:4). Christ is the one "that is able to keep you from falling, and to present you faultless before the presence of his glory." Not only can He do it, but He also enjoys doing it "with exceeding joy" (Jude 24)! Every Christian can rest assured that his faithful High Priest and the Holy Spirit are praying for his protection from the world, the flesh, and the Devil (John 17:15; Romans 8:26–27; Hebrews 7:24–25).

---

[1]N2H2 Incorporated, "N2H2 Reports Number of Pornographic Web Pages Now Tops 260 Million and Growing at an Unprecedented Rate," *PRNewswire-First Call*, September 23, 2003, http://ir.thomsonfn.com/ InvestorRelations/PubNewsStory.aspx?partner=6269&layout=ir_ newsStoryPrintFriendly.xsl&storyid=94774.

[2]Stan Keller, "Where Can I Get Help for My Growing Problem with Internet Pornography?" *The Parsonage*, 2004, http://www.family.org/ pastor/faq/a0011334.html.

[3]"FBI to Parents: Internet Pedophiles a Serious Threat," *CNN Interactive*, March 11, 1998, http://www.cnn.com/TECH/computing/9803/11/cyber. stalking/.

ITS
PERVERSITY
3

He said furthermore unto me, Son of man, seest thou what they do? even the *great abominations* that the house of Israel committeth here, that I should go far off from my sanctuary? but turn thee yet again, and thou shalt see *greater abominations.* (Ezekiel 8:6)

And he said unto me, Go in, and behold the *wicked abominations* that they do here. So I went in and saw; and behold every form of creeping things, and abominable beasts, and all the idols of the house of Israel, pourtrayed upon the wall round about. (Ezekiel 8:9–10)

He said also unto me, Turn thee yet again, and thou shalt see *greater abominations* that they do. (Ezekiel 8:13)

Then said he unto me, Hast thou seen this, O son of man? turn thee yet again, and thou shalt see *greater abominations* than these. (Ezekiel 8:15)

Then he said unto me, Hast thou seen this, O son of man? Is it a light thing to the house of Judah that they commit the abominations which they commit here? for they have filled the land with violence, and have returned to provoke me to anger: and, lo, they put the branch to their nose. (Ezekiel 8:17)

great abominations

greater abominations

wicked abominations

greater abominations

greater abominations

Abominations

In Ezekiel's vision, God repeated certain phrases to emphasize how wicked and depraved Israel had become.

Before we discuss the extreme content of the Dark Side of the Internet, let's take a quick look at this word *abomination* in the Bible. We know that it is a broad word that encompasses everything that God hates. The sin of immorality is not the only sin that is an abomination in the eyes of God. When we truly love someone, we learn to hate what he hates. This is part of the great Bible doctrine of the fear of the Lord. Part of fearing God is hating what He hates and loving what He loves. What is it that God hates? What is a true abomination in God's eyes? Is there anything that has crept into our lives and thinking that is actually an abomination in God's eyes? Search your heart as you read through the following verses:

God's List of Abominations

> These six things doth the Lord hate: yea, seven are an abomination unto him: A proud look, a lying tongue, and hands that shed innocent blood, An heart that deviseth wicked imaginations, feet that be swift in running to mischief, A false witness that speaketh lies, and he that soweth discord among brethren. (Proverbs 6:16–19)

A Proud Heart

> Every one that is proud in heart is an abomination to the Lord: though hand join in hand, he shall not be unpunished. (Proverbs 16:5)

Lying Lips

> Lying lips are abomination to the Lord: but they that deal truly are his delight. (Proverbs 12:22)

Wicked Thoughts

> The thoughts of the wicked are an abomination to the Lord: but the words of the pure are pleasant words. (Proverbs 15:26)

Making Bad Look Good, and Good Look Bad

> He that justifieth the wicked, and he that condemneth the just, even they both are abomination to the Lord. (Proverbs 17:15)

The Worship and Lifestyle of the Wicked

> The sacrifice of the wicked is an abomination to the
> Lord: but the prayer of the upright is his delight. The
> way of the wicked is an abomination unto the Lord: but
> he loveth him that followeth after righteousness.
> (Proverbs 15:8–9)

Involvement with the Occult

> When thou art come into the land which the Lord thy God
> giveth thee, thou shalt not learn to do after the abomina-
> tions of those nations. There shall not be found among
> you any one that maketh his son or his daughter to pass
> through the fire, or that useth divination, or an observer of
> times, or an enchanter, or a witch, Or a charmer, or a con-
> sulter with familiar spirits, or a wizard, or a necromancer.
> For all that do these things are an abomination unto the
> Lord: and because of these abominations the Lord thy
> God doth drive them out from before thee. (Deuteronomy
> 18:9–12)

Tons of information available online can easily be classified as abominable to God. The Dark Side of the Internet is a never-ending evil. It is
extreme in its content. It never quits! It gets more disgusting and more
deviant the deeper you dig. For years we have been warned of the evils
of television, which certainly hosts a tremendous amount of wickedness
offered as "entertainment." But in comparison to the Internet, television
has standards. For instance, unless someone subscribes to a wicked adult
cable channel, he cannot watch X-rated shows on TV. But every type of
perverted wicked immorality is available online.

Online Dangers

What are the dangers for you? What are the dangers for your future
children? What are the dangers for your future husband or wife?

Easy and Anonymous Access to Pornography

Easy and anonymous access to pornography is a great danger. The
Internet has decreased the hurdle of shame that comes with purchasing
pornographic magazines and materials. It used to be dirty old men
sneaking around adult bookstores, but now that has all changed. The
wicked bookstores have sneaked into your homes. Could you imagine
your mom saying, "Hey, could you run down to the store and get a
gallon of milk and maybe a box of Oreo cookies . . . double stuffed."
So you do. You go down to the grocery store and pick up the milk, get

the cookies, and while you are there you purchase a pornographic magazine. You go home, drink the milk, eat the cookies, and flip through the magazine with your mom. I don't think so! Why not? Mom's there! But why do so many teens go to their room, shut the door, make sure nobody is around, and start surfing wicked Internet sites?

Do you realize that the pornography that is legally restricted to adults can be accessed by *kids*? A few clicks of a mouse and any child, of any age, can poison his mind. Unless parents use disciplinary and technical safeguards (such as filters or filtered ISPs), they are allowing an open-door policy to all sorts of perversion not only into their homes but also into the very hearts of those they love so much. Parents, brothers, sisters, and friends must all be willing to warn of the poisonous snakes that are ready to strike. We must lovingly protect young children from this kind of evil that will prey upon their sin nature by feeding it before they have the intellectual or spiritual maturity to deny their lusts.

The Severity of Internet Pornography

The Internet is home to countless images that would be illegal to sell even in adult bookstores. When God shared with Ezekiel the phrases *great abominations, greater abominations,* and again, *greater abominations,* He was emphasizing the fact that His people seemingly had no limits—the unrestrained, unlimited, uncontrolled involvement in the most wicked of all abominations. The New Testament has an old English word that is used for this unbridled sin—*lasciviousness.* Lasciviousness is sin without restraint. Sin without boundaries. Sin without limits. It is an attitude of life that promotes no authority or absolutes. It is the attitude of mind that says, "Nobody—absolutely no one—is going to tell me what to do, not even God!" Lasciviousness breaks the heart of God. Men who promote this unrestrained lifestyle deny God, hate God, and have hardened their hearts against God. Carefully meditate on the following verses that deal with this wicked philosophy of life:

> For from within, out of the heart of men, proceed evil thoughts, adulteries, fornications, murders, Thefts, covetousness, wickedness, deceit, lasciviousness, an evil eye, blasphemy, pride, foolishness: All these evil things come from within, and defile the man. (Mark 7:21–23)

> And lest, when I come again, my God will humble me among you, and that I shall bewail many which have sinned already, and have not repented of the uncleanness and fornication and lasciviousness which they have committed. (2 Corinthians 12:21)

> Now the works of the flesh are manifest, which are these; Adultery, fornication, uncleanness, lasciviousness, Idolatry, witchcraft, hatred, variance, emulations, wrath, strife, seditions, heresies, Envyings, murders, drunkenness, revellings, and such like: of the which I tell you before, as I have also told you in time past, that they which do such things shall not inherit the kingdom of God. (Galatians 5:19–21)

> This I say therefore, and testify in the Lord, that ye henceforth walk not as other Gentiles walk, in the vanity of their mind, Having the understanding darkened, being alienated from the life of God through the ignorance that is in them, because of the blindness of their heart: Who being past feeling have given themselves over unto lasciviousness, to work all uncleanness with greediness. (Ephesians 4:17–19)

> That he no longer should live the rest of his time in the flesh to the lusts of men, but to the will of God. For the time past of our life may suffice us to have wrought the will of the Gentiles, when we walked in lasciviousness, lusts, excess of wine, revellings, banquetings, and abominable idolatries: Wherein they think it strange that ye run not with them to the same excess of riot, speaking evil of you. (1 Peter 4:2–4)

For there are certain men crept in unawares, who were
before of old ordained to this condemnation, ungodly
men, turning the grace of our God into lasciviousness,
and denying the only Lord God, and our Lord Jesus
Christ. (Jude 4)

The Distribution of Child Pornography

In reference to child pornography, I want to be as discreet as I possibly
can. We have got to understand the seriousness of the spiritual warfare
we are engaged in. My personal ministry necessitates many hours face
to face with teenagers whose hearts have been crushed and minds have
been polluted because of sexual abuse. I cannot even tell you the number of times I have sat with teenagers whose dads, stepdads, brothers,
or moms' boyfriends have sexually abused them in some fashion. It
rips your heart out! One teen girl shared with me that her mom's
boyfriend raped her and now she lives with the terrible complications
of AIDS. Another girl told me that her stepdad raped her and not only
did she get pregnant, but she was also forced by her mom to have an
abortion. We must understand that every single time there is any child
pornography online—*every time*—some child's life has been destroyed.
Some child's life has been wrecked! Yes, and it could be your little
sister or your little brother. It could be your son or daughter someday.
And still, so many professing Christians are choosing to download
such wickedness.

The Dark Side of the Internet has
become a stalking place for perverted
men—a playground for child molesters. This is not a secret to police de-
partments or news agencies, but it
seems to be to many moms and dads.
In the book *Safety Net: Guiding and
Guarding Your Children on the
Internet*, Chapter 4 is entitled "Why
Is the Internet a Pedophile Playground?"[1] An article from ABC
News entitled "Stalking Internet
Pedophiles" describes an undercover
cybercop who posed as a child porn
producer. He went to a chatroom
where men trade in child pornography and met a twenty-one-year-old
student preparing to be (get this) a

kindergarten teacher. These men meet in chatrooms, send their images back and forth, and in this case, encourage the further abuse of children by increasing the demand for new images.[2] Whoa! Can you believe how wicked men can get?

> Many people are shocked to learn that it has been estimated that approximately 1 in 3 girls and 1 in 7 boys will be sexually molested before age 18. The typical serial child molester will abuse more than 360 victims over the course of his lifetime. He is able to abuse 30–60 children before he is even caught for the first time.[3]

It is common knowledge among authorities that the majority of convicted child molesters are regular users of pornography.[4] Many people say, "Come on, that will never happen to me. Where I live it is absolutely no problem." In a Focus on the Family publication, a mom explains how the Dark Side of the Internet affected her family and life. She writes,

> I've always felt that pornography was bad, that it was harmful. But I felt that it didn't affect me personally. No members of my family ever read pornography. My husband's family didn't read pornography. We live in a small, close-knit community. Pornography is not an issue there. I basically felt immune to its effects. A year ago in April, my world was shattered by the effects of pornography. My three-year-old daughter was raped and violated in every manner you can imagine by a twelve-year-old boy. When they arrested the young man, we were told that they would surely find sexual abuse in his background. And that this is the reason he

did it on my daughter. After a thorough psycho-sexual evaluation, they came to one conclusion. There was a single motivating factor in what he did to my baby. He was exposed to pornography at a very vulnerable time in his life. What he saw on those pages not only gave him the ideas of what to do and how to do it, but it gave him the permission to treat females in a degrading and debasing manner. Since he was only twelve years old, he needed to look for a female who was younger than him, who wouldn't fight back. And so he raped and molested my daughter. I've heard it said that pornography is a victimless crime. I'm standing here before you a victim of pornography. My little girl is a victim of pornography.[5]

Entrapment by the Pornographers

Teens have confessed to me that open, unfiltered, unlimited access to the Internet, especially its Dark Side, is one of the greatest struggles they face.

> Pornographers prey upon the depraved lusts in us all.
> (cf. James 1:14)

Let me explain the dangers. All the pornographers want is money. That's it. They don't care about you. They don't care about God. Pornographers know that all they need to do is to reach out that ugly claw of pornography, grab hold of an inquisitive or innocent mind, and they've got you! You are trapped! Pornographers prey upon the depraved lusts in us all. I talked to a teenaged boy recently who was doing a homework assignment online with his mom sitting right by his side. He and his mom have no idea how the porn appeared on the screen—but there it was. They immediately turned the monitor off and rebooted their computer. The fourteen-year-old boy told me that he had never seen anything like it before or since—but he wanted to. Seeing the image just one time locked into his mind and created the desire for more. You might be innocently checking scores or working on a paper for school, and something will come on the screen that you know is sinful. Maybe a bad pop-up appears, or perhaps you unknowingly click a link to a bad site. You may even say, "Man, that's bad!" But the next day, you want to go back and see some more. That is how powerful this trash is.

So what do the pornographers do? They seek to captivate a teen's heart through high-tech temptation. They have tried using sites that look like what you want until you click on them and realize that you are in the wrong place. They know the most prominent sites that kids or teens will visit for fun or homework assignments and try to trick them into clicking the wrong link. Some pornographers have studied the most common misspellings and word orders, so if you mistype something or put the wrong ending on an Internet address—boom— here comes the filth on the screen.[6]

Availability of Violent Entertainment

> Then he said unto me, Hast thou seen this, O son of man? Is it a light thing to the house of Judah that they commit the abominations which they commit here? *for they have filled the land with violence,* and have re-turned to provoke me to anger: and, lo, they put the branch to their nose. (Ezekiel 8:17)

Ezekiel 8:17 mentions that the house of Judah *filled the land with violence.* When violent behavior, which shows absolutely no regard for human life, becomes our daily entertainment, we are not far off from returning to the mentality of Roman culture. Almost every type and form of violence can be found online—from making bombs to joining terrorist groups worldwide.

Computer games, such as Doom and Duke Nukem, were highly publicized by the Peducah, Kentucky (December 1997) and Littleton, Colorado (April 1999) high school killings. The boys involved in the shootings not only played those games but also used the Internet to gain information on how to make bombs. Both the graphic violence and incredibly wicked content of games like these have helped to desensitize teens and kids into thinking violence is just another way of hav- God hates ing fun. For example, in the game Postal 2, play- violence! ers "go postal" and get points for killing innocent bystanders and police.

God hates violence! He always has. When God was grieved be-cause of the wickedness of man, it was the violence on the earth that prompted the destruction of the world with the Flood.

> The earth also was corrupt before God, and the earth was filled with violence. And God looked upon the earth, and, behold, it was corrupt; for all flesh had corrupted his way upon the earth. And God said unto Noah, The end of all flesh is come before me; for the earth is filled with violence through them; and, behold, I will destroy them with the earth. (Genesis 6:11–13)

> By the multitude of thy merchandise they have filled the midst of thee with violence, and thou hast sinned: therefore I will cast thee as profane out of the mountain of God: and I will destroy thee, O covering cherub, from the midst of the stones of fire. (Ezekiel 28:16)

God asked Ezekiel in Ezekiel 8:17,

> Is it a light thing to the house of Judah that they commit the abominations which they commit here? for they have filled the land with violence, and have returned to provoke me to anger.

Is it a *light* thing, is it no big deal, doesn't it matter to us that we choose for entertainment that which God hates? Those who view graphic violence as fun or entertaining are like the people of Ezekiel's day who *provoked God to anger.* Never forget the admonition of the writer of Hebrews 10:31 when he said, *"It is a fearful thing to fall into the hands of the living God."*

---

[1]Zachary Britton, *Safety Net: Guiding and Guarding Your Children on the Internet* (Eugene, OR: Harvest House, 1998).

[2]Michael J. Martinez, "Stalking Internet Pedophiles," *ABCNEWS.com*, September 2, 1998, http://more.abcnews.go.com/sections/tech/dailynews/pedophiles0217.html.

[3]Gene Abel, quoted in "Battle Against Pornography," *The Parsonage*, 1999, http://www.family.org/pastor/resources/sos/a0006443.html.

[4]Tim Graham, "House Members Are Lining Up with Anti-Child Porn Bill," *World*, May 25, 2002, http://www.worldmag.com/world/issue/05-25-02/national_1.asp.

[5]"Diane," quoted in "Fact Sheet: Pornography's Permeation in a Sexually-Saturated Society," *The Parsonage*, 1999, http://www.family.org/pastor/resources/sos/a0006443.html.

[6]"Fact Sheet #7: Is Pornography So Easy to Find on the Internet?" www.enough.org/New.Porn.on.net.html (accessed November 24, 2003). Additional information can be seen on www.enough.com and www.protectkids.com.

ITS
PRIVACY
4

> Then said he unto me, Son of man, hast thou seen what
> the ancients of the house of Israel do in the dark, every
> man in the chamber of his imagery? for they say, The
> Lord seeth us not; the Lord hath forsaken the earth.
> (Ezekiel 8:12)

"Nobody will ever find out what I am doing. I can cover my tracks.
I mean, really, who will know? I'm here all alone at home; nobody is
watching; I know enough to delete my trail. Am I not entitled to my
own privacy in my own home?"

People Will Find Out

There is no privacy. The Internet offers only a false sense of privacy.
Somewhere, sometime those choosing to be involved in this sin will
be found out.

A teenaged boy walked up to me, and as he asked if we could
talk, broke into tears. One thing he loved to do after school was to
sneak home and scare his dad in his home office. This teen would
quietly sneak up to the office window, bang on the window, and
scream—scaring his dad out of his wits. One night after school, the
boy followed his normal routine and went to scare his dad; only this
time just before he screamed, he looked into the office window at his
dad's computer screen and could not believe what he saw his dad
viewing. The boy knew it had to be a pop-up or something and
waited for his dad to get rid of it. Instead, his dad connected to more
filthy sites. Not really knowing what to do, the boy ran inside to his
mom and they both went to the office door, which was locked. By the
time they got inside the office, the computer had been turned off and
the boy's dad denied everything. In sharing his
tragic story with me, the boy looked up at me
and said, "The problem is, he's not just my dad;
he's also my pastor, and I don't know what to
do." There is no privacy. Delete does not mean
delete. Your secret sins may not be as secret as
you think they are.

> Your secret sins
> may not be as
> secret as you
> think they are.

I once talked to a police secretary that deals with all the sex offense crimes in her area. She told me the list of those caught is so
long that they do not know how they can deal with each case. She
also mentioned that years ago they would deal with the sex offenders
and always find they were victims of sexual abuse in the past. Now,
almost all the cases are motivated by Internet pornography. Pornography use is exposed.

While preaching at a men's retreat, I heard the story of a very
successful businessman who was tempted while working online in
his office. (This man was a Christian leader with a Christian family.)
Instead of resisting the temptation, he clicked on to the website and
spent a few minutes viewing the pornography and then returned to the
same site some time later. What he did not know was that the company monitored employees' Internet activities. Because this company
had zero percent tolerance for pornography (as all companies should),
the man was dismissed from his high-paying job. The story does not
end there. There were ramifications at home and at church too.

Secret sins may not be as secret as many think they are. Now
remember, no believer *has* to sin and give in to these temptations. A
young youth pastor shared with me that while doing some research
online for a sermon, all of a sudden there was obscene material on
the screen. Not knowing what to do, he started screaming for the sec-

retary to come in. She ran in and
both started unplugging everything
in the office—yes, the computer,
the copier, the phones, the coffee-
maker—everything. Even though
that may have been a bit much, at
least the others in that ministry
knew that the youth pastor was not
trying to hide anything. He, like
Joseph in the face of temptation,
ran the only way he knew to run.

A seventeen-year-old girl came
to me and asked if we could talk.
When I asked what she was strug-
gling with, she immediately started
to weep. As she wept she shared
this story.

A few weeks ago I went to check my e-mail—and you know how you can sometimes just type in two or three letters and the URLs will come up? Well, that's what I did, and when I hit Enter I could not believe what was on the screen. It was more wicked and filthy than I could have ever imagined. I got so mad. I knew it couldn't be my dad. He was a deacon in our church and a Christian school teacher. I knew it wasn't my mom; she doesn't even know how to boot up the computer. I didn't think it could have been my older sister in a Christian college, but she had been home a few weekends. I figured it had to be my friend who spent a weekend with me. So I called my friend and got all over her case about why she would do that on our computer! My friend said, "I didn't do that." So I waited two more weeks for my sister to come home and I confronted her. She simply looked at me and said, "I didn't do that." Now I don't know what to think . . . but it's got to be my dad.

I asked the girl if she could talk to her dad. She said, "No." I asked her if she would like for me to talk to him. She responded, "Would you, please?" So that night I sat in my office and called his home. Without letting him defend himself or make excuses, I basically gave him the same story that his daughter gave me—how she tried so hard to prove that it could not be him. At the end of the conversation I said, "Sir, either someone's sneaking into your house in the middle of the night watching this filth on your computer or you have got a problem." He was very quiet for a long time and then he responded, "I struggled with my thought life for many years. And now it's just too easy."

There is no privacy, none. I'm not a computer geek, but I understand that there are many ways that a computer can record where you have been and what you have accessed. Websites can keep track of visitors and gather information about them. You say, "Not me; I know how to delete all the temporary Internet files and cookies." Go ahead! In fact, smash your computer with the biggest sledgehammer you can find and then throw it into the deepest lake around;

Zach didn't know his ISP had records too.

31

you can still be tracked. Your Internet Service Provider knows where you have been. There is no privacy.

You might say, "Come on, who cares? Who cares about me? Who would even want to know?" Satan. The Devil not only wants to entrap you, but he also wants to expose you. If he can make a Christian look weak and wicked, he is actually telling the world that the Christian does not serve a very powerful God. He is showing an unsaved world that God's holiness means nothing to that Christian. He wants to make God look very foolish in the eyes of the world.

God Knows

Many today think like the individuals in Ezekiel 8:12: "For they say, The Lord seeth us not; the Lord hath forsaken the earth." God is not watching. He doesn't really care about what I'm doing. He's got the whole world to run; what does He care about me?

Look at Ezekiel 8:12 again. "Then said he unto me, Son of man, hast thou seen what the ancients of the house of Israel do in the dark, every man in the chamber of his imagery? for they say, The Lord seeth us not; the Lord hath forsaken the earth." This may startle some and annoy others, but there is no privacy.

Slowly read through the following verses three times. *Think*, so you can understand what God says about those who try to hide their sin in the dark. *Concentrate*, to see what God says about secret sins. *Meditate*, to see that there is no privacy—none.

> For the eyes of the Lord run to and fro throughout the whole earth, to shew himself strong in the behalf of them whose heart is perfect toward him. Herein thou hast done foolishly: therefore from henceforth thou shalt have wars. (2 Chronicles 16:9)

> The eye also of the adulterer waiteth for the twilight, saying, No eye shall see me. (Job 24:15)

> There is no darkness, nor shadow of death, where the workers of iniquity may hide themselves. (Job 34:22)

> Thou hast set our iniquities before thee, our secret sins in the light of thy countenance. (Psalm 90:8)

> Yet they say, The Lord shall not see, neither shall the God of Jacob regard it. Understand, ye brutish among the people: and ye fools, when will ye be wise? He that

planted the ear, shall he not hear? he that formed the eye, shall he not see? (Psalm 94:7–9)

For the ways of man are before the eyes of the Lord, and he pondereth all his goings. (Proverbs 5:21)

The eyes of the Lord are in every place, beholding the evil and the good. (Proverbs 15:3)

For God shall bring every work into judgment, with every secret thing, whether it be good, or whether it be evil. (Ecclesiastes 12:14)

Woe unto them that seek deep to hide their counsel from the Lord, and their works are in the dark, and they say, Who seeth us? and who knoweth us? (Isaiah 29:15)

For mine eyes are upon all their ways: they are not hid from my face, neither is their iniquity hid from mine eyes. (Jeremiah 16:17)

Can any hide himself in secret places that I shall not see him? saith the Lord. Do not I fill heaven and earth? saith the Lord. (Jeremiah 23:24)

For there is nothing hid, which shall not be manifested; neither was any thing kept secret, but that it should come abroad. (Mark 4:22)

For the eyes of the Lord are over the righteous, and his ears are open unto their prayers: but the face of the Lord is against them that do evil. (1 Peter 3:12)

Even if the world never knows, even if your mom and dad never find out what you have been doing in the dark, even if someday your spouse never suspects anything, even if your boss has no clue, even if you keep it hidden from those who respect you the most, *God knows*! It is He that you are sinning against. It is His holiness that you are forgetting. Never forget the promise of God's watchful eyes.

God knows!

God Sees the Heart

By Ron Hamilton and Jamie Langston Turner

Our God measures man by a standard divine,
For He sees underneath ev'ry outward design.
He looks past possessions and costly attire;
He studies the heart—every thought and desire.

Our God does not judge by how tall we may stand,
Or how much we possess, or the rank we command.
His gaze goes far deeper to things that endure;
He honors the man who keeps his heart pure.

For the eyes of the Lord are searching to and fro.
We have no secrets that our God does not know.
Our Father knows our thoughts; He understands ev'ry part.
Man sees the outside, but God sees the heart.

ITS
PRICE TAG
5

Then he said unto me, Hast thou seen this, O son of man? Is it a light thing to the house of Judah that they commit the abominations which they commit here? for they have filled the land with violence, and have returned to provoke me to anger: and, lo, they put the branch to their nose. Therefore will I also deal in fury: mine eye shall not spare, neither will I have pity: and though they cry in mine ears with a loud voice, yet will I not hear them. (Ezekiel 8:17–18)

No one can sin and win! We can choose our sin, but we cannot choose the consequences of our sin. Play with fire and you will get burned. Play this game and you will lose: you'll lose your testimony . . . you'll lose trust from your parents . . . you'll lose your purity of mind . . . you'll lose trust from your future husband or wife . . . you'll lose a close relationship with the Lord . . . you will lose!

Internet Relationships

While Satan uses visual images to attract and attack men, he uses the lure of fantasy-relationships to destroy women and girls. The numbers of inappropriate relationships are steadily rising. Think about some of the wicked girls in the tragic and sordid tales of the Old Testament: Lot's daughters and Gomer. None of these situations seemed to be sudden acts of passion; all were premeditated acts designed to change the circumstances of life in which they found themselves.

> No one can sin and win! You will lose!

Let's take a few minutes and think about e-mail and chatrooms. A *U.S. News & World Report* article states, "Five girls sit side by side in a Baltimore middle school library, typing away at the PCs, eyes riveted to their screens. 'We're emailing each other,' one blurts out. Never mind that they could just talk; chatting in cyberspace is far better." [1] There is something exciting about sitting down and typing away to your friends. The same article also states, "Children send a goodly portion of the 403 million IMs that go out every day, discussing who's cool . . . and other similar matters." [2]

Communication has reached a new level with IMs (Instant Messages), e-mail, online chatting, and probably ten more new ways to communicate before this book is even published. It's a brand new world of communication and it changes every single day. It is also very dangerous.

In all the research that I have seen to date, I have found absolutely *nothing* good about public chatrooms.

- You don't know who you're talking to.
- You don't know when you're being lied to.
- You meet people you would never hang out with in real life.
- You say things you would never say in person.
- You can get pulled into conversations without even realizing where you are headed.
- You waste tons of time.

"So, what school do you swim in?"

I recently received this e-mail from a concerned teenaged boy.

> I caught my dad a couple of months ago chatting with another lady. I followed a couple of history trails and found that he had been sending her Internet e-cards, which were kinda mushy. I approached him about it and he said that he made a mistake and it was over. I trusted him that it was. Last week I walked by the computer, and I saw him typing [an] e-mail to someone. Rand, I am really struggling right now. My parents are both Christians and they have raised me well. I really love my dad and I don't want to lose him to something stupid.

An article in *U.S. News & World Report* titled "Saturday Night and You're All Alone?" illustrates how chatting and online romance can change a life.

> [Question:] How is cyberdating different from meeting at a club?
> [Answer:] It's a lot different. Everybody in cyberspace is tall, thin, blond, and rich—at least in theory. . . .
> [Question:] I met this woman on the Net two months ago. She thinks I'm "Cowboy," a daring Hollywood stuntman. But really I'm just a quiet, skinny account-ant. Now she wants a face to face. Help![3]

The July 15, 1993 edition of *The New Yorker* (page 61) presents a famous cartoon that has a mangy-looking dog typing away on the Internet. The caption on the bottom of the cartoon says, "On the Internet, nobody knows you're a dog."

> Cyber-romance can strain a marriage, sometimes to the breaking point. One woman, an attractive professional in her mid-30s, compares chat rooms to the temptation of drugs. Her husband's clandestine four-month Internet romance with a married woman living in an-other state nearly wrecked their 10-year marriage. . . . When she asked him why their monthly bill for using the Net exceeded $200, she says, her husband told her, "I'm in love with the perfect woman and I'm leaving you." His "true love" was planning to leave her hus-band, but plans changed following an out-of-state tryst. "Each of them thought the other was the greatest— until they actually met," the woman says. Her husband begged to come back. She relented, and they're now in marriage counseling.[4]

Seldom does a week go by that I do not hear about another sad situation where lives are destroyed by involvement in the Dark Side of the Internet. Here is one such story. We'll call the girl Kayla.

Kayla was a great kid. She was active in her church and was home schooled. She was very shy and not a bit boy crazy. She never gave her folks any problems. Kayla's dad woke up at three one morn-ing, knowing something was wrong. He went to Kayla's bedroom and she wasn't there. Scared, he quickly woke up his wife. They prayed and then went to call the police because they didn't know what to do. Just before they picked up the phone to call, they heard the door open downstairs. Kayla came up the steps, and what they learned they could not believe. You see, because Kayla was such a good kid, she was allowed to surf the web and go to chatrooms without any filters, totally unsupervised. Because she was so shy, it was very hard for her to talk to boys. But online, she became pretty bold and met a guy that she enjoyed chatting with. For a while, she was smart enough not to tell him anything about herself or who she was. But then they got to the point where they were asking questions such as, "Do you like me? I like you. It's been fun talking," and so forth. They started to get very filthy in their talk and very wicked. Finally, he talked her into sending him her phone number so they could meet face to face. The problem was this other "kid" was a twenty-nine-year-old married man. But because they had talked for so long and built such a friendship, she agreed to meet. Also, because they had talked so dirty for so long, it was easy for him to talk her into sleeping with him, and she did. Obviously, the parents were heartbroken.

Internet Addiction

Sin is very expensive. The price tag on online sin is out of sight. This tool not only destroys homes and innocent victims, but it also addicts with unbelievable power.

There are many names given for those addicted to the web—netheads, cyberfreaks, Webaholics, chat junkies, and mouse potatoes.

The Internet has brought distractions into cubicles, and now corporate America is fighting back. Consider what a *Newsweek* article called "CyberSlacking" says,

> There's Gamesville.com, a game-playing site with the slogan, "Wasting your time since 1996." . . . And then there's DonsBossPage.com, a Dagwood Bumstead-style site filled with jokes and games that gets 5,000 hits a day. Each site features a prominent panic button in case

the boss wanders by. Simply click on it and a phony spreadsheet pops onto your screen and typing sounds clack from your speakers.[5]

Christians cannot afford to regard their lusts as petty: lusts are the beginning of susceptibility to temptation from without, and sin, and ultimately death. To say you are above this kind of thing is to deceive yourself; self-deception is to be expected from sinful hearts (Jeremiah 17:9; 1 John 1:8–10). What is a little lust today can tomorrow be your downfall. James writes,

> But every man is tempted, when he is drawn away of his own lust, and enticed. Then when lust hath conceived, it bringeth forth sin: and sin, when it is finished, bringeth forth death. (James 1:14–15)

> **God forgives, but He does not promise to remove the consequences of sin.**

God forgives, but He does not promise to remove the consequences of sin. Sin hurts. Sin is very painful. Sin has consequences that dog us the rest of our lives. The ultimate price someone pays when he chooses to be involved in what God hates is God's displeasure and anger. This is a price too great to pay.

[1]Marc Silver and Joellen Perry, "Youngsters Get Hooked on Instant Messages," *U.S. News & World Report*, March 22, 1999.

[2]Ibid.

[3]Beth Brophy, "Saturday Night and You're All Alone?" *U.S. News & World Report*, February 17, 1997.

[4]Ibid.

[5]Keith Naughton, "CyberSlacking," *Newsweek*, November 29, 1999.

ITS PREVENTION

6

> Then I beheld, and lo a likeness as the appearance of
> fire: from the appearance of his loins even downward,
> fire; and from his loins even upward, as the appearance
> of brightness, as the colour of amber. And he put forth
> the form of an hand, and took me by a lock of mine
> head; and the spirit lifted me up between the earth and
> the heaven, and brought me in the visions of God to
> Jerusalem, to the door of the inner gate that looketh
> toward the north; where was the seat of the image of
> jealousy, which provoketh to jealousy. And, behold, the
> glory of the God of Israel was there, according to the
> vision that I saw in the plain. (Ezekiel 8:2–4)

What can you do? How can you prevent such wickedness from
destroying you? What is the prevention to avoid the Dark Side of the
Internet? First of all, look at one phrase from the passage above,
"Behold, the glory of the God of Israel." Behold, look at, observe,
learn about, concentrate on *the glory of God*! God's glory involves all
that He is, His power, His mercy, His might, His strength, His long-
suffering, His holiness, and His greatness. When you study and learn
who God is and *what* He is like, you learn to fear Him. In a practical
way, you learn to begin hating what He hates and loving what He
loves. The more time you spend with God, the more you will learn
about Him. The more you know about Him, the more you will love
Him. The more you love Him, the more you will have a wholesome
dread of displeasing Him. Your love for God will prevent you from
choosing to be involved with that which God hates. Your fear of God
will keep you from the abominations of God. Meditate on the following passages of God's Word:

> Whether therefore ye eat, or drink, or
> whatsoever ye do, do all to the glory of
> God. (1 Corinthians 10:31)

> I will praise thee, O Lord my God, with
> all my heart: and I will glorify thy name
> for evermore. (Psalm 86:12)

In a practical way,
you learn to begin
hating what He
hates and loving
what He loves.

> Trust in the Lord with all thine heart; and lean not unto thine own understanding. In all thy ways acknowledge him, and he shall direct thy paths. Be not wise in thine own eyes: fear the Lord, and depart from evil. (Proverbs 3:5–7)

> Keep thy heart with all diligence; for out of it are the issues of life. Put away from thee a froward mouth, and perverse lips put far from thee. Let thine eyes look right on, and let thine eyelids look straight before thee. Ponder the path of thy feet, and let all thy ways be established. Turn not to the right hand nor to the left: remove thy foot from evil. (Proverbs 4:23–27)

> The night is far spent, the day is at hand: let us therefore cast off the works of darkness, and let us put on the armour of light. Let us walk honestly, as in the day; not in rioting and drunkenness, not in chambering [immorality] and wantonness, not in strife and envying. But put ye on the Lord Jesus Christ, and make not provision for the flesh, to fulfil the lusts thereof. (Romans 13:12–14)

What can you do now? Daniel purposed in his heart not to defile himself with culturally accepted behavior. Make up your mind that you will not allow this evil to destroy your heart and life. The following four practical Bible principles can help you hate what God hates and love what He loves. These Bible truths will help you remember that whether you eat, drink, or spend time online, you can do *all to the glory of God*!

The "Secret Agent" Principle

> Let the words of my mouth [chatrooms and e-mail: the things I say], and the meditation of my heart [thought life: the things I think], be acceptable in thy sight, O Lord [Everything I think, everything I say, Lord, I want to be acceptable in Your sight.], my strength, and my redeemer. [By Your strength, Lord, I can and will have victory.] (Psalm 19:14)

Secret agents think that they can sneak around and never be seen. They think they are almost invisible. Don't fall for that! Don't try to hide. Don't try to be a spiritual secret agent hiding from God. Don't try to hang on to secret sins. There are three Bible principles to help keep you from becoming a secret agent—accountability, visibility, and vulnerability.

Prevention Guide for Internet Usage

The "Secret Agent" Principle
Let the words of my mouth, and the meditation of my heart, be acceptable in thy sight, O Lord, my strength, and my redeemer. (Psalm 19:14)

- Accountability: Never go online alone.
- Visibility: Never surf in secret.
- Vulnerability: Never talk to strangers. Refuse to give any personal information of any kind to anyone.

The "Surfer Dude" Principle
A prudent man foreseeth the evil, and hideth himself: but the simple pass on, and are punished. (Proverbs 22:3)

- Refuse to surf aimlessly—it will keep you out of deep water.
- Know where you are going and what you want.

The "Sumo Wrestler" Principle
But put ye on the Lord Jesus Christ, and make not provision for the flesh, to fulfil the lusts thereof. (Romans 13:14)

- Protect with passwords.
- Protect with filters or a filtering ISP.
- Protect with the Delete button.

The "Strange Woman" Principle
Remove thy way far from her, and come not nigh the door of her house: Lest thou give thine honour unto others, and thy years unto the cruel: Lest strangers be filled with thy wealth. (Proverbs 5:8–10)

- Concentrate on your relationship with your family.
- Concentrate on your future relationship with your spouse.
- Concentrate on your relationship with God.

Accountability

Never go online alone. Make sure your mom, dad, a brother, or a sister is there. Have a friend over; invite the entire junior and senior class from school to your house! Do whatever is necessary to stay accountable. Accountability is having someone around to keep you from falling or to help pick you up after you have fallen. Solomon put it this way:

> Two are better than one; because they have a good reward for their labour. For if they fall, the one will lift up his fellow: but woe to him that is alone when he falleth; for he hath not another to help him up. Again, if two lie together, then they have heat: but how can one be warm alone? And if one prevail against him, two shall withstand him; and a threefold cord is not quickly broken. (Ecclesiastes 4:9–12)

Who knows where you go on the Internet? Who keeps checks on you on a regular basis? Accountability partners are true friends. Two are better than one to keep us as far away from sin and temptation as possible. If your mom and dad constantly check up on you, be very thankful. If they love you that much to keep you from messing up your life, you've got parents who really care.

Setting up accountability partners takes a ton of commitment and reveals a pure heart that wants to avoid the sins involved in the Dark Side of the Internet. For example, at least one company offers a filter option that involves an accountability report.[1] When you set up this filtering system, you choose three friends: a parent, a co-worker, a spouse, a secretary, a fiancé, or a true friend that is not afraid to confront you if you make some stupid choices in this area. These three "accountability friends" will receive a weekly e-mail that lists all the Internet sites you went to or attempted to go to. That is great accountability.

You donated to the S.P.C.S.?!?
(Society for the Prevention of Cruelty to Shrimp)

Well, yes and no...

Accountability partners will help keep you from going where you shouldn't.

Visibility

Never surf in secret. Please pay attention to this principle. If you truly have a heart for God and you don't want to blow your mind and your life on the trash available on the Dark Side of the Internet, please, get the computer out of your bedroom. Put it in a place where others constantly walk by. Don't allow it to be in a place where you can be all by yourself, where you think no one can see. If your computer is out in the open where parents and siblings are around, it will help keep you from falling into a "secret sin." Here are a few verses from a previous chapter:

> The eye also of the adulterer waiteth for the twilight, saying, No eye shall see me. (Job 24:15)

> Thou hast set our iniquities before thee, our secret sins in the light of thy countenance. (Psalm 90:8)

> For God shall bring every work into judgment, with every secret thing, whether it be good, or whether it be evil. (Ecclesiastes 12:14)

> Woe unto them that seek deep to hide their counsel from the Lord, and their works are in the dark, and they say, Who seeth us? and who knoweth us? (Isaiah 29:15)

> For mine eyes are upon all their ways: they are not hid from my face, neither is their iniquity hid from mine eyes. (Jeremiah 16:17)

> Can any hide himself in secret places that I shall not see him? saith the Lord. Do not I fill heaven and earth? saith the Lord. (Jeremiah 23:24)

> For there is nothing hid, which shall not be manifested; neither was any thing kept secret, but that it should come abroad. (Mark 4:22)

Vulnerability

Never talk to strangers. Do you remember when you were a little kid and your mom would say, "Never talk to strangers"? Well, don't do it online. Chatting is dangerous business because you don't know who you're talking to! Do not set yourself up to be hurt. You may say, "Come on, I'm not stupid! I'll be careful!" You don't have to be stupid to get into trouble on the Dark Side of the Internet. For instance, there was a girl living in a small town who was "not stupid." She met a guy online and continued to chat with him. She was careful not to give him a name, phone number, e-mail address, or any information where he could contact her. She was just having some fun. She did not share anything, well, almost anything. She did say that she loved softball and told him she was number "7." She also mentioned that they were going to play their rival team on Friday night and mentioned the name of the team! Well, the guy was not an idiot—he simply did his research, found out where the schools were, went to the game, and approached number "7" after the game. She couldn't believe he found her. He talked her into stopping for a bite to eat on the way home. She went with him and was raped.

You don't have to be stupid! Please, don't try to be a secret agent. Remember our three principles. Accountability: Never go online alone. Visibility: Never surf in secret. Vulnerability: Never talk to strangers.

The "Surfer Dude" Principle

A prudent man foreseeth the evil, and hideth himself: but the simple pass on, and are punished. (Proverbs 22:3)

This verse is a warning from God. A *prudent* man will never choose to be an Internet surfer dude. Prudence has the connotation of being cautious and looking ahead in order to stay out of trouble. A prudent man carefully obeys all signs that warn, "Beware." A prudent person listens to warnings and attempts to stay as far away from sin and temptation as he can.

The wisdom of the prudent is to understand his way: but the folly of fools is deceit. (Proverbs 14:8)

The simple believeth every word: but the prudent man looketh well to his going. (Proverbs 14:15)

When a *prudent* teen or adult goes online, he will be careful in what link he follows or which site he visits. If it *might* be a problem, he stays away. The prudent *forseeth the evil*; he wisely sees the problem in time to get out of there. You could say that he forseeth and fleeth. He *hideth himself.* A New Testament principle is tied to the Bible word *flee.* Note this word in the following verses:

Flee fornication. Every sin that a man doeth is without the body; but he that committeth fornication sinneth against his own body. (1 Corinthians 6:18)

Wherefore, my dearly beloved, flee from idolatry. (1 Corinthians 10:14)

> But thou, O man of God, flee these things; and follow after righteousness, godliness, faith, love, patience, meekness. (1 Timothy 6:11)

> Flee also youthful lusts: but follow righteousness, faith, charity, peace, with them that call on the Lord out of a pure heart. (2 Timothy 2:22)

The word *flee* has the idea of being a fugitive, to run so far and so fast that you cannot be found. What did Joseph do when he was tempted by Mrs. Potiphar? He fled, he ran, he got out of there. The *prudent* man knows how to *flee.*

Now, let's look at the *simple.* To illustrate this word, consider the translation of it in the Septuagint (the Greek translation of the Hebrew Scriptures), *aphrones,* which basically means "unthinking." Some would translate the Hebrew word "naive." You're not thinking, you're incredibly naive, if you think you can mess with the Dark Side of the Internet and escape the judgment of God.

Aphrones–Proverbs 22:3

"The simple pass on, and are punished" (Proverbs 22:3). The simple don't think! Wow, that looks good! Let's click on there! The simple minded lack both discernment and discretion to stay away from sin. The simple do not take the time to weigh out the consequences of their actions against the temporary thrill they may receive.

> How long, ye simple ones, will ye love simplicity? and the scorners delight in their scorning, and fools hate knowledge? (Proverbs 1:22)

> And beheld among the simple ones, I discerned among the youths, a young man void of understanding. (Proverbs 7:7)

> A foolish woman is clamorous: she is simple, and knoweth nothing. (Proverbs 9:13)

Be prudent! Think! Refuse to be simple minded. Think before you go online; think while you are online; think about where you were online. Think! Think! Think!

> *Refuse to surf aimlessly—it will keep you out of deep water.*

Never go online just to hang out.

Never go online just to hang out. Refuse to surf aimlessly! If you go online to check some scores or sales and then start surfing around without knowing where you are going, you had better be careful what wave you catch. Do you catch one kind of Internet wave while Mom or Dad is in the room and another kind of Internet wave when nobody is watching? Refuse to surf aimlessly. It will keep you out of deep water where you could drown yourself in all kinds of sin and wickedness.

Know where you are going and what you want.

Have a destination in mind. Make a shopping list of what you need and where you think you can find it. In fact, surfing the web is quite a bit like shopping. Guys, if you would go online like you shop, you would be fine. As you know, guys shop differently from girls. When a girl shops, it's like she's on a mission. For instance, a girl needs a blouse to complete her new outfit. She goes to a fancy clothing store like Wal-Mart. She walks into the store. As soon as she passes the smiling greeters, she sees a rack on sale—98 percent off—and the first blouse she picks up is her size; it is her color; it costs only a nickel! But she has to look at every other blouse in the store before she buys that one. And then she has to go to another store.

Now men shop like a Special Forces operation. Locate target. Strike. Retreat. That's it. Get in there, get what you want, and get out of there! If guys would go online with the same mindset, they would have a much better chance of being called *prudent* rather than *simple.*

The "Sumo Wrestler" Principle

> But put ye on the Lord Jesus Christ, and make not provision for the flesh, to fulfil the lusts thereof. (Romans 13:14)

Sumo wrestlers are, well, sumo wrestlers. I would not like to look like one (as much as six or seven hundred pounds), but I'd love to eat like one. When they compete, they get in the middle of their fighting circle and they wrestle. One of the ways they can lose is if they get pushed or bumped out of the circle. They are fighting in dangerous territory when they wrestle too close to the edge of the circle.

In regards to the Dark Side of the Internet, don't live on the dangerous "edge" of the circle. Stay in the middle. A God-pleasing life is not living on the "edge" of worldliness and wickedness, where one small slip means disaster. It is staying as far away from sin as you can. And by the way, don't just stay away from sin—stay away from temptation. "Lord, lead us not into temptation." Stay as far away from it as you possibly can. This is where the Bible principle from Romans 13:14 applies.

"Put ye on the Lord Jesus Christ." Put on His character. Put on His characteristics. Learn to be Christlike. Make your goal in personal purity and lifestyle to be as Christlike as you possibly can. Paul's admonition does not stop there. Put on Christlike characteristics and do not make "provision[s] for the flesh, to fulfil the lusts thereof." In other words, do not provide a way to satisfy the intense passions and desires of this wicked flesh. Do not plan to sin. Do not creatively devise a way to cover your sinful tracks. Make it hard to sin! Set up such established boundaries that you will have to consciously say "no" to an accountability friend, "no" to a family member, and "no" to God in order to sin.

Stay in the middle of the wrestling ring. Do not flirt with sin. Stay as far away as you can. This principle can apply to any worldly temptation you face. Think about it. Some might say, "You can't tell me that this outfit I am wearing is unbiblical!" They may be right! I might not have a chapter and verse, but it looks so much like the world; it is so close to the "edge" that I want to stay as far away as I can. Some want to argue about their choices in music. They may say, "You can't tell me that God's Word speaks expressly against this style of music!" Again, I may not find a specific Bible verse; but much of today's popular music, even in Christian circles, looks and sounds so much like the world; it is so close to the "edge" that I want to stay away. What about physical involvement in dating? The thousand-dollar question is "How far can I go?" That is living on the edge! That kind of thinking will lead only to defeat and disaster. It is not "How far can I go and still be OK?" The question should be "How pure can I be?"

> It is not "How far can I go and still be OK?" The question should be "How pure can I be?"

I love McDonald's french fries. No, I *love* McDonald's french fries. But if I ate McDonald's french fries every day of my life, I would look like a super-sized Happy Meal—and I don't want that! So

I'm going to stay away! In regards to the Dark Side of the Internet, you need to stay as far away from temptation as possible. How do you do that?

Protect with passwords.

If you are consumed with pleasing and glorifying God, then push yourself away from the "edge" with passwords. (This assumes your access to the Internet is by dial-up. Unfortunately, you don't need a password with cable or DSL.) Ask Mom to put in the password so you cannot go online without her at home.

A creative way to protect yourself and your family is to split a password. After you are married, split a password with your spouse. Determine right now that when you do find that special person, you will insist on splitting a password in your home. Don't say, "Well, I trust him." We shouldn't trust ourselves! Split a password. Let's give an example.

Split passwords make it harder to sin.

Suppose a young couple agrees to split a password for their Internet access. The husband sits down at the computer, trying to think of a good password to remember. His wife has decorated the kitchen in apples, so he types in "apple." He leaves and his wife sits down at the computer. She knows that her husband's favorite meal is fritters. So she types in "fritters." She does not know "apple" and he does not know "fritters." About two weeks later, the young husband comes home from work to find a note from his wife left on the door saying that she is shopping and won't be home until later that night. As he walks by the computer he is tempted. He sits down at the keyboard and types in "apple." He thinks, "Now what would she have been thinking? 'Applesauce,' no, that's not it. 'Apple-jacks,' no, wrong again." For this young husband, no "fritters," no Internet. No "fritters," no sin.

Protect with filters or a filtering ISP.

Not only passwords but also filters will help to protect you and your family. There are all kinds of filters you can purchase and put on your computer. But even better than filters, protect yourself with a filtering ISP—Internet Service Provider. The most popular ISPs, such as AOL or MSN, have limited filtering capabilities and statistically host many of the adult-oriented sites available. You need to find an ISP that filters out the objectionable material before it ever gets to your home. Research to find the one that best suits your needs.[2] If you carefully study your area to see what is available, you will find an ISP that will work for you to help protect every member of your family. If you're not able to choose your ISP (which is often the situation if you have cable or DSL instead of dial-up) and your ISP does not filter sites very well, then you need to purchase a good filter. It is crazy to have unfiltered Internet access in your home! You might as well dump a dozen poisonous snakes in your living room than to have Internet capabilities in your home with no filter. Don't live on the "edge." Stay as far away from temptation and defeat as you possibly can.

Some have argued, "There are no filters that take care of everything!" They are right! But shouldn't you take care of as much as you can? Some things will get by even the best of filters, but a good percentage of objectionable sites will be blocked. With millions of pages coming online each week, there is no way any filter can catch all the bad ones. (Sometimes, even with a good filter, you can still innocently access a bad site.) Even when most bad sites are blocked, if you really want to get at something objectionable, you can. But you will have to climb over the fence and bust the door down to get there. At that point, you are making a choice. Of course, since fallible filters can't get everything, you need a variety of preventive measures. Filters or a filtering ISP can help keep you from slipping, but they are not foolproof. (You should also look into installing a pop-up blocker.) All these technical safeguards need to be combined with disciplinary safeguards.

Protect with the Delete button.

One more area of protection is the use of the Delete button on your keyboard. You may get an e-mail from a pornographic site wanting you to see what they offer. Delete it without ever opening it up. In fact, if you get an e-mail and you are not sure who the sender is, delete it! If someone really needs to contact you, he can still call you on the telephone.

What if the pornographers have tapped into your e-mail address and you are daily faced with those disgusting ads? First, never, never go to any of their sites, or they will send your e-mail address world-wide. Second, if they have already found you, close out your account and start a new account with a completely different e-mail address. Some will think that is too much of a hassle, but losing a family member to the evils of the Dark Side of the Internet is much worse. Some people have two e-mail addresses—one that's given out to family and friends, and one that's used with online businesses. If your business e-mail address is sold to a bad company, you can drop it more easily. Third, consider purchasing a spam filter, which will filter out at least some of the bad stuff.

In this section I've discussed some technical safeguards. But don't blindly trust in them; they're just aids to help you. Since they're not perfect and since you won't always be in situations where they are in place, you need to have personal safeguards. You need to make up your mind that *you* will take responsibility for where you surf and not rely on technology.

The "Strange Woman" Principle

Remove thy way far from her, and come not nigh the door of her house: Lest thou give thine honour unto others, and thy years unto the cruel: Lest strangers be filled with thy wealth. (Proverbs 5:8–10)

Our last principle in fighting the evils of the Dark Side of the Internet is called the "strange woman" principle. Slowly read the passage the above verses came from:

Hear me now therefore, O ye children, and depart not from the words of my mouth. Remove thy way far from her, and come not nigh the door of her house: Lest thou give thine honour unto others, and thy years unto the cruel: Lest strangers be filled with thy wealth; and thy labours be in the house of a stranger; And thou mourn at the last, when thy flesh and thy body are consumed, And say, How have I hated instruction, and my heart despised reproof; And have not obeyed the voice of my teachers, nor inclined mine ear to them that instructed me! (Proverbs 5:7–13)

Proverbs 5:8 says, "Remove thy way far from her, and come not" near the icon of her website (in application this is a great way to look at this verse). Stay away! Do not allow yourself to get close to her territory.

Proverbs 5:10 states, "Lest strangers be filled with thy wealth." If you take a little rectangle piece of plastic and type in a series of four numbers, another series of four numbers, and do the same two more times ending with an expiration date in order to purchase pornography with your credit card, you are headed for spiritual destruction. You are a time bomb waiting to explode. Never buy sin! Refuse to give your money to wicked men. The pornography business is all about money. If no one bought it, it would not exist. Never let these wicked strangers be filled with your wealth.

Proverbs 5:9 reads, "Lest thou give thine honour unto others, and thy years unto the cruel." Concentrate on what you are about to read. Your pastors, your teachers, your mom and dad have lived a life built on good decisions, serving God for maybe twenty-five years. Twenty-five years of raising godly kids that are in a Christian college. Twenty-five years of doing what is right. Twenty-five years of good choices and clean living. Twenty-five years! Then one night—one night of foolish choices and involvement with the Dark Side of the Internet. Only one night, but that night they get caught. What do people remember of them? The twenty-five years of right choices? No. The one night of sin. God forgives, but many never forget. Do not throw your years away "unto the cruel."

Concentrate on your relationship with your family.

Guys, before you ever click on a pornographic site, think what it would be like if after twenty minutes of poor choices, you were so engrossed in what you were seeing you did not hear your mom standing in the doorway with tears streaming down her cheeks. Think about how much it will hurt your mom. I have had moms call me because they are concerned that their sons or husbands are messing around with this Internet trash. Do you know what I spend time doing while you're at school? Over the telephone, I've talked to moms, helping them find out where you have been online. Some would say, "That's not fair." Yes, it is. The best thing in the world for those involved in the Dark Side of the Internet is to get caught.

Concentrate on your future relationship with your spouse.

Many of you hope to be married in the next ten, twenty, thirty, or forty years. Hey, guys, do you want to marry a girl who during her teenage years was talking dirty to other guys? Is that the kind of girl you want to marry? I don't think so. Girls, do you want to marry a guy who during his teenage or college years was constantly watching pornography on-line? Is that the kind of guy you want to be a father to your little girl someday? I don't think so. Faithfulness to a wife or a husband involves the way we think as well as the way we act.

Concentrate on your relationship with God.

> Draw nigh to God, and he will draw nigh to you. Cleanse your hands, ye sinners; and purify your hearts, ye double minded. (James 4:8)

God told Ezekiel in his vision that His people have . . .

> . . . turned their backs on Me

> . . . driven Me out of My sanctuary

> . . . chosen to be involved with the things that I hate

> . . . literally pushed Me out of their lives.

My Prayer for You

Dear reader, my prayer for you is that these statements are never said about you. Don't turn your back on God. Don't drive God out of your life. Don't choose to be involved with things that God hates. Don't literally push God out of your life. God wants the best for your life. Please, don't get caught in the Dark Side of the Internet.

[1]American Family Association (AFA) offers this filtering system as of early 2004. Please refer to http://www.bjup.com/textbooks/resources for suggested resources.

[2]Please refer to http://www.bjup.com/textbooks/resources for filters and ISP suggestions.

CHRISTIANS, THE WORLD, AND CULTURE

Introduction to the Essays

You're probably thinking, What on earth are all these essays? More importantly, Why should I take the time to read them? These essays are written to challenge your thinking about a number of questions. Avail yourself of the help they offer. Some are loosely related to each other. Reading them all will give you a well-rounded look at the issues; however, each may be read alone.

Essay 1, **"The Bible and the Internet,"** asks how we may legitimately interpret the Bible to apply it to modern-day questions about the Internet.

Essay 2 discusses a more specific problem: **"Temptation."** What is it, what does the Bible say about it, and how do we handle it? The essay follows David's life and sin with Bathsheba as a case study.

Essay 3, **"Christians and Culture,"** traces the concept of culture through Genesis 1–11 and advocates a basic, biblical approach for relating to culture.

Essay 4, **"Our Quest for Consistency,"** offers a broad look at the many ways people in Christendom have thought about culture. It offers an array of questions to help you think consistently about the many cultural questions you face.

Essay 5, **"Beyond Content Issues,"** asks questions about the nature of the Internet itself—the Internet as a phenomenon in culture. How does the Internet affect culture and individuals?

THE BIBLE AND THE INTERNET

by Thomas Parr

Do you think it's foolish to write a book on what the Bible says about the Internet? The Bible doesn't even mention the Internet. So aren't those who write such a book adding to Scripture (Mark 7:7)? Isn't it wrong to go beyond what is written (1 Cor. 4:6)? Doesn't God threaten people who go beyond what He has said (Deut. 4:2; 12:32; Rev. 22:18–19)? How can we prove we are not simply using the Bible as a club and forcing people to conform to man-made standards?

These are all very important questions since they basically ask how relevant the Bible is to modern times. The Bible does not explicitly mention many behaviors that harm and destroy homes today: child abuse, smoking, drug use, pornography, and a slew of other problems. So, is the Bible sufficient, or isn't it? Is it able to help us deal with all the perplexing problems we face today?

Should You Care?

Many people don't even care about these issues. They're not concerned about the issues of our day, and they don't care about the Bible's relevance or sufficiency. These people either do not have a Christian worldview or do not live consistently with one. However, the Bible clearly states that Christians should live their lives according to its teachings. They are to view the world the way the Bible does and to behave in keeping with its perspective (see Ps. 1:1–2). Gaining this biblical worldview requires hard work and diligence.

> My son, if thou wilt *receive* my words, and *hide* my commandments with thee; So that thou *incline* thine ear unto wisdom, and *apply* thine heart to understanding; Yea, if thou *criest* after knowledge, and *liftest up* thy voice for understanding; If thou *seekest* her *as silver*, and *searchest* for her *as for hid treasures*; Then shalt thou understand the fear of the Lord, and find the knowledge of God. (Proverbs 2:1–5)

Reading the Bible once is not enough to help a person live in a way that pleases God. The Bible must permeate a person's thinking through constant exposure (Josh. 1:8). Far from finding Scripture to be dull, those who meditate in it "all the day" (Ps. 119:97) find it a "delight" (Ps. 1:2; 119:35). The obstacle to this, of course, is as Jesus warned: "cares and riches and pleasures" choke out the Word of God in people's lives (Luke 8:14). If a life given to pursuing God through His Word seems dull to you, it is probably because you love something else more than you love God.

So, is the Bible sufficient? The question is not whether the Bible is authoritative. Any consistent Christian would affirm its authority. The question is, *Does the Bible provide all the moral direction necessary for us to make choices that are pleasing to God in every situation*? As we experience the nearly limitless possibilities and decisions life offers, can the Bible provide direction for it all? Many Christians today deny that the Bible does actually provide this kind of guidance. They assert that the Bible gives only the vaguest general principles and that applying them to issues of our times almost always results in distorting those principles. In their view, God is silent about many questions we face in life, and we are left to figure them out alone.

In answer, we must ask the all-important question, What does the Bible itself say about its sufficiency? If the Bible, which is our only source for discovering God's mind, answers this issue for us, then the matter is settled. The Bible is the authority, so we must find out what it says about itself.

Is God's Word Sufficient?

Consider the following passage from 2 Timothy:

> All scripture is given by inspiration of God, and is profitable for doctrine, for reproof, for correction, for instruction in righteousness: That the man of God may be perfect, throughly furnished unto all good works. (2 Timothy 3:16–17)

Let's examine these verses closely, because at first glance they don't seem to say anything about the Bible's ability to guide us in every circumstance. The text clearly establishes the authority of Scripture when it says that all Scripture is inspired by God. This phrase is a translation of the Greek word *theopneustos*, which means "breathed out by God." The source of the words of Scripture is God Himself, not man. If God's Word were somehow mixed with autonomous human thought, then what it says about eternity, heaven, the final judgment, salvation, and even the character of God would be suspect. Humans have no way of knowing anything for certain about the spiritual realm unless someone from that realm tells them. And the person from that realm must be truthful, omniscient, and able to subject all things to His will in order to guarantee anything. In other words, for man to know anything authoritatively and objectively true about spiritual reality, he must receive communication from an omniscient God (Ps. 147:5; 1 John 3:20) who cannot lie (Titus 1:2) and who works all things after the counsel of His will (Eph. 1:9). And that is exactly what this passage says we have in Scripture. Man has received communication that has supreme authority over him because it is *God's Word.*

Because the Bible is God-breathed, it is therefore "profitable" for four things. First, it is profitable for "doctrine," that is, teaching. The Bible is profitable to teach us truth. Without the Bible, we would be cut off from truth, and we would dwell in a relativistic world in which human opinion jockeys for ascendancy. Without the authoritative Word, we would be left with, "Well, so-and-so says this, but the other guy says the opposite." Thankfully, we are not in this situation. We can go to Scripture and say, "Thus saith the Lord," because the Bible is God-breathed and valuable for teaching us absolute truth.

Second, the Bible is profitable for "reproof," or showing us where we are wrong. Though this may sound negative, listen to God's breathed-out viewpoint of the matter: "It is better to hear the rebuke of the wise, than for a man to hear the song of fools" (Eccles. 7:5). Since God's Word is completely authoritative and always right, it therefore functions perfectly as the standard by which to judge all of our actions. Whatever God has proclaimed to be good is good. Whatever He has proclaimed to be evil is evil. Woe to him who mixes up the two (Isa. 5:20). We learn to distinguish good from evil through God's Word. Without His Word, we would be abandoned to a morally subjectivistic world in which everyone's opinion about morality would be as valid (or invalid) as everyone else's. But with God's Word we can compare ourselves with the inerrant standard and see where our lives and thoughts do not measure up. Humanistic man has no such benefit. He is left without a reference point for morals or logic and thus cannot justify moral or logical assertions. Truly the Scriptures are "better . . . than thousands of gold and silver" (Ps. 119:72).

Third, God's Word is profitable for "correction." What benefit is there in being reproved if we aren't corrected? It would be like a teacher showing a student all his mistakes but never showing him how to fix them. The Bible gives us God's divine viewpoint on how to correct our fallen behavior.

Fourth, God's Word is profitable for "instruction." This Greek word *paideian* apparently refers to the training needed to ingrain corrections so that they become second nature. God's Word doesn't simply hit the nail on the head once; it repeatedly hammers the nail of truth until it is firmly lodged in our conscience and in our life. All we must do is expose ourselves to its sanctifying influence (Ps. 119:9–11).

What is the purpose of God's giving us an authoritative and thus profitable revelation? Second Timothy 3:17 says that God's Word will make a person "perfect," which means here to make something well-fitted to a task. What task? The next phrase answers, "throughly furnished unto all good works." In modern English it would say, "completely equipped for every good work." In other words, God's Word has been given to us to fit us for the task of accomplishing every good deed. *This necessarily implies that the Bible gives us the resources to distinguish good and evil in every circumstance.* This answers our original question: Is God's Word sufficient for guiding us in every circumstance? Yes, the Bible was given to completely equip us for *every good work.*

Sufficiency in Our Times

Of course, the Bible does not address every modern issue. So how can it give us direction in areas that it speaks nothing about?

In Matthew 22:29–33, Jesus helps us answer this question. A number of the Sadducees (a Jewish religious group that denied the resurrection and believed only the Pentateuch to be inspired) related to Jesus a scenario about a woman who had been married seven times because her husbands kept dying. At the end of her life she had had seven husbands, and then she herself died. "In the resurrection whose wife shall she be?" the Sadducees asked Jesus, thinking they had proved the impossibility of the resurrection. Jesus answered with the following:

> Ye do err, not knowing the scriptures, nor the power of God. For in the resurrection they neither marry, nor are given in marriage, but are as the angels of God in heaven. But as touching the resurrection of the dead, have ye not read that which was spoken unto you by God, saying, I am the God of Abraham, and the God of Isaac, and the God of Jacob? God is not the God of the dead, but of the living. And when the multitude heard this, they were astonished at his doctrine. (Matthew 22:29–33)

Jesus' answer was twofold. First, he showed that one of their pre-suppositions was wrong. In their argument against the resurrection, they assumed that the afterlife is similar to this life—that marriage relationships remain the same. Their entire argument against the resurrection depended on this presupposition. But Jesus explained that the afterlife does not involve marriage. So the whole basis for their objection was faulty.

Second, he argued for the resurrection from the Pentateuch, the section of the Old Testament they accepted. Essentially, He told them that they should have inferred from Exodus 3:6 that there is an afterlife and a resurrection. Jesus' logic goes something like this: God spoke of Abraham, Isaac, and Jacob as though they still existed after their deaths; therefore, there must be an afterlife and a resurrection. Though there is no explicit statement in the Pentateuch concerning a resurrection, the Sadducees should have read it between the lines. In other words, Jesus expected them to draw inferences from Scripture.

Facts That Support Christ's Use of Exodus 3:6

Deuteronomy 1:8 says that God swore to give the land (of Canaan) to Abraham, Isaac, Jacob, *and* to their seed. Genesis 17:8 says that God was going to give the land to *both* the patriarchs *and* their descendants *forever*. But the patriarchs never received the land. Did God fail to keep His promise to those Old Testament men? Only if there is no resurrection. These verses from the Pentateuch lead a person to expect exactly what Hebrews says Abraham conceived of—a resurrection from the dead (Heb. 11:19). God's Word still stands— the patriarchs themselves will possess the land forever.

Consider the inferences that Jesus expected the Sadducees to make. First, Jesus quotes Exodus 3:6: "I am the God of . . . Abraham, the God of Isaac, and the God of Jacob." Then follows a number of possible inferences required to reach the conclusion that there will be a resurrection from the dead (the first inference Jesus stated explicitly; the rest are implied): (a) God is not the God of the dead but of the living; (b) therefore, Abraham, Isaac, and Jacob were alive after they died; (c) since it is impossible to consider the promises given to the patriarchs (e.g., Gen. 17:8) as remaining unfulfilled forever, one day these patriarchs will be reunited with their bodies. The words of Exodus 3:6 alone do not address the Sadducees' rejection of resurrection. *Christ expected them to combine biblical statements with logical inferences to come to the right conclusion. He expected them to reason scripturally.*

Those who want to find God's will in the Bible do this all the time. They instinctively see places in Scripture that parallel a particular issue they are facing, and they apply that Scripture verse or passage to their situation.

For example, a high school student is tempted to smoke cigarettes. He happens to be a Christian student with a strong desire to please God, but those who want him to smoke say that there's nothing wrong with it. And when he responds that it is not the Christian thing to do, they sneer and assert that the Bible doesn't mention smoking; so, they say, it isn't wrong. Are the students right? Is the Christian student a prude and a Pharisee? The godly student searches the Scriptures in order to discover God's mind on the subject and finds 1 Corinthians 6:19–20.

> What? know ye not that your body is the temple of the Holy Ghost which is in you, which ye have of God, and ye are not your own? For ye are bought with a price: therefore glorify God in your body.

Considered in their original context, these verses were given to combat the Corinthians' tolerance of sexual immorality (see the previous verses). But the principle that our bodies are holy and therefore we must not harm or defile them (see also 1 Cor. 3:17) also applies to situations other than sexual immorality. With the modern medical understanding that smoking is harmful to bodily health, it is logical to apply 1 Corinthians 6:19–20 to smoking and to any activity that is physically harmful.

The process with the smoking issue is similar to what we saw in Matthew 22. A Christian faces a question about whether smoking is OK: (a) 1 Corinthians 6:19–20 teaches that we should glorify God in our bodies because the Holy Spirit dwells in them; (b) as we know from medical science, smoking is harmful to our bodies; (c) it would not be glorifying God in our bodies to purposefully harm them (cf. 1 Cor. 3:17); (d) therefore, smoking is not a proper activity for a Christian.

Avoiding Wacky Inferences

It is very possible to make both good inferences from Scripture and very poor inferences from Scripture. Many of us can recall a time when someone we knew made an inference from a passage, and we thought, how did he get that point from that passage? We must be careful to explain the scriptural reasoning behind our inferences. If we don't, even if our inference is biblical, others may not be able to tell that it is. A teacher of God's Word must use the truth as Solomon described. "The words of the wise are as . . . nails fastened by the masters of assemblies, which are given from one shepherd" (Eccles. 12:11). The truth needs to be fastened into people's minds and hearts. A hesitant blow is not enough to convince. Truth needs to be fixed firmly by sound scriptural reasoning.

So how do we keep from making unconvincing or even faulty inferences? How do we fasten the truth into our own minds and others'? The following discussion gives some basic principles.

Get the Big Picture: How to Reason Scripturally (or how to make proper inferences)

1. Know your Bible generally.

2. Know the context, historical background, and original intent of specific passages you want to apply.

3. Demonstrate that the text legitimately applies to the situation today.

4. Understand as much of the modern issue as possible.

5. Be careful not to contradict a clear statement of Scripture.

6. Let the Bible interpret itself and direct its own applications.

7. Pray for the Holy Spirit's illumination.

First, you must *know your Bible generally.* Consider as a negative example a man who once sincerely stated that King Solomon was an African. For proof he went to a statement from the Song of Solomon:

"I am black" (1:5). Are you perplexed, knowing that Solomon was David's son by Bathsheba (both of whom were Semitic in descent)? Go to the passage and read it. After a cursory reading, you should easily discern that the statement was not from the lips of Solomon but from his betrothed. Also, the word *black* in ancient Israel did not necessarily connote being of African descent as it does in modern America. As a matter of fact, the context of the passage seems to indicate that it simply referred to being darkened by the sun, i.e., having a suntan (cf. 1:6). The man who thought that Solomon was African probably thought that since the name of the book was "The Song of Solomon," every word in it was Solomon's. He also assumed that the words in the Bible have only the meaning that he instinctively ascribed to them at first sight. Both of these errors are the mistakes of one to whom the Bible is foreign. A person who is this biblically illiterate should not be making inferences. If he tried, he would be wrong more often than not.

Second, you must *know the context, historical background, and original intent of specific passages you want to apply.* Many people have used the biblical statement found in Genesis 31:49 to comfort a loved one who is going to be away from home: "The Lord watch between me and thee, when we are absent one from another." Sounds very spiritual and comforting. However, in their original context these words were never intended to convey this meaning. They are the words of Laban to Jacob, and they actually convey the idea of "May the Lord keep an eye on you while I can't." A careful reading of the context will reveal that these words were spoken by a suspicious and greedy man who was afraid of Jacob's taking advantage of him. Misunderstanding a passage's context results in misunderstanding God and believing things you think are from Him but are really products of your imagination.

It is not theologically disastrous to use Genesis 31:49 to comfort, for example, a departing college freshman who will be away from home for the first time. But getting in the habit of using Scripture without regard for historical background and context can be disastrous. There are many important Christian doctrines that can be maintained only because of careful evaluation of the progress of a passage's argument. If you never strive to follow those arguments, you will always fail to discover some of the Bible's greatest riches and may even fall into grievous error.

Third, once you understand the context, historical background, and original intent of a passage, you can (and must!) *demonstrate that the text legitimately applies to the situation today.* Matthew 7:1,

"Judge not, that ye be not judged," may be one of the most misapplied verses in the Bible, because people don't understand why it was spoken to begin with. Therefore, they are unable to perceive its legitimate modern-day application. People apply it to oppose those who make morally discerning statements. And often this application is followed by a snide, "Who are *you* to tell *me* I'm wrong?" Can this application be demonstrated as legitimate?

What does the context indicate? Verse 1 gives the command to not judge. Verse 2 gives a reason for not judging: the same standard you use to judge others will be used to judge you. If a person reads only to this point in the passage, there would be nothing to dissuade him of the erroneous interpretation given in the previous paragraph. "No one has the right to judge anyone else, because we're all sinners, and judging people will only aggravate our condition."

But the logical flow of the passage does not end with verse 2. Jesus goes on, clarifying several points. Verses 3–5 basically explain that it is impossible to rightly correct a minor flaw in someone's life when you yourself have a major flaw in your life. This gives a clue as to whom Jesus is addressing in this discussion of judging. He is addressing those who are totally insensitive to the massive, log-like spiritual problems in their own lives and yet are hypersensitive to others' slight, speck-like problems. Verse 5 actually commands you to judge another person's problems—only after you get your own life right. So the context makes the common application of verse 1 impossible. Jesus is commanding people who do not have their lives right with God to refrain from judging, because judging others will only aggravate their condition. Get your life right first, and then you will see clearly enough to properly judge others without condemning yourself.

Matthew 7:1 therefore does not address a person who exercises moral discernment. Rather, it applies to hypercritical people who make condemning judgments of other people's flaws without seeing their own. Those who misuse Matthew 7:1 do so because they do not understand the verse in context and therefore cannot demonstrate that their application is valid to the modern issue at hand.

Fourth, you must *understand as much of the modern issue as possible.* This often requires an accurate understanding of medical issues involved, such as, for example, knowing that smoking is physically harmful. Without that piece of medical knowledge, the whole previous argument against smoking breaks down. Understanding an issue also often requires an accurate knowledge of the historical background of the situation (a necessity in evaluating the phenomenon of rock music, for example). Fully understanding an issue also requires knowing the facts about the issue as it stands at present in today's society. Often this is one of the first steps a person must make even before evaluating a specific passage.

Fifth, you must *be careful not to contradict a clear statement of Scripture* in your inference or application. For example, Scripture repeatedly tells God's people to discriminate between truth and error (Matt. 7:15–16; 1 Cor. 2:15; Eph. 5:10; 1 Thess. 5:21). Thus, anyone who says Matthew 7:1 forbids discernment is contradicting these clear statements. The Pharisees in Mark 7:10–13 had a spiritual-sounding rule about consecrating resources to the Lord so that they wouldn't have to use those resources for their aging, needy parents. However, although dedicated to the Lord, those resources were still in the possession of and were being used by the original owner. So people were using money selfishly under the guise of devotion to God while their neglected parents were in need. Thus the Pharisaical rule sounded spiritual but actually avoided obeying God's command to honor one's parents.

Sixth, *let the Bible interpret itself and direct its own applications.* The strongest inferences or applications are those that are bolstered by obviously parallel passages from elsewhere in the Bible. Recall in the Matthew 22 issue that the inference made from Exodus 3:6 is more understandable and acceptable when considered in the light of Genesis 17:8 and Deuteronomy 1:8. Notice also how 1 Corinthians 3:17 assisted in applying 1 Corinthians 6:19–20 to the smoking issue.

Finally, *pray for the Holy Spirit's illumination.* Without the Spirit's ministry of opening our minds, we will never be able to apprehend truth. Never assume that saved people don't need to pray for illumination. God's people in the Old and the New Testaments have always depended upon God in this way (Ps. 119:27; Eph. 1:15–18). We are spiritual morons without the Spirit's ministry (1 Cor. 2:14), so beseech God to "open thou mine eyes, that I may behold wondrous things out of thy law" (Ps. 119:18).

Making proper inferences from Scripture requires consistent and persistent searching of Scripture. Those who are unfamiliar with the whole counsel of God will inevitably make poor inferences. Happily, however, familiarity with Scripture can increase; and with hard work and heartfelt prayer, our wisdom in walking the way of the Word can also increase.

What do you think of the following inferences? Defend your conclusions with Scripture, observations from context, and scriptural reasoning. Do not pronounce the following inferences wrong based on your personal preferences. Do not judge until you've done your research and have a strong scriptural case. Do not accept anything by what it appears to be on the surface. Many of these require quite a bit of research. Some are less demanding. Some of the statements below are damning heresies (5, 6, and 9 have historically been understood as such). Others are wrong, though they do not condemn a person to hell for believing them. All face serious biblical challenges.

1. Matthew 5:39: "We as individuals must never fight back against those who do violence." (pacifism)

2. Matthew 5:48: "We are able to become perfect in this life." (perfectionism)

3. Mark 10:21: "If we want to follow Jesus, we are obligated to sell everything we own."

4. Matthew 23:9: "We must never call anyone 'Father' in this life except God."

5. Mark 14:22–24: "The bread and wine in Communion become the literal body and blood of Jesus." (transubstantiation)

6. Ezekiel 33:15: "People have the ability within themselves (without assistance from God) to choose and please God." (Pelagianism)

7. 1 Corinthians 9:22: "Just as Paul did, we must sacrifice our standards for the sake of evangelism. Nothing is more important than people getting saved."

8. Galatians 5:18: "The Old Testament moral law has no authority over Christians. We do not need to keep those laws." (antinomianism)

9. James 2:24: "The Bible explicitly teaches that a man is justified before God by doing good things. God accepts people into heaven on the basis of their good deeds in this life." (works salvation)

Encountering the Modern Issue Before Encountering the Text

Often, Christians are confronted with modern issues first and then must begin hunting for passages to help them deal with those issues. The problem that this approach presents is that it is all too easy to latch onto a passage that, after further study, turns out to be either unrelated or only semi-related to the problem at hand. The questions we are asking now are, *When we are faced with an issue we have not evaluated before in the light of Scripture, how do we find passages that directly apply to the issue we are facing?* and *How do we demonstrate that the passages apply?*

The answer to both questions is that we must understand and explain the modern issue in the light of a general, Christian view of the world. Often, people don't know how to apply passages to problems in the world because they don't understand the world itself. God made the world, completely understands it in its sinful state, and has given us clear testimony in Scripture about it. If we do not comprehend that testimony, then we will fail to know the world as it really is. Christians must understand basic truths about the world and man's sinful nature that are true in every age. Failure to do this often results in some degree of misapplication. Since the modern issue we are discussing is the Internet, we must relate the Internet to the rest of the world that God created. The following discussion essentially does the fourth step above: *Understand as much of the modern issue as possible.* (Essays 3, 4, and 5 will also help fill out your understanding of the modern issue.)

The World

Failure to know the Bible's perspective of our world results in our failing to understand our world as it really is, which results in our inability to justify our choice of passages to apply in life. After considering the following principles, we will be able to view the Internet more precisely from God's perspective.

The Greek word that is most often translated *world* in the KJV is the word *kosmos.* It has a number of possible meanings, depending on the context. It can mean the globe in space on which we dwell (John 21:25; Acts 17:24); the mass of humanity (John 1:29); or human society or culture as organized against God (John 15:19; 17:6, 9, 14; 1 Cor 1:21; 11:32).

One very interesting and illuminating use of *kosmos* is found in 1 Peter 3:3: "Whose adorning [*kosmos*] let it not be that outward adorning of plaiting the hair, and of wearing of gold, or of putting on of apparel." Here Peter uses the word to describe the arrangement of a woman's apparel, actually her whole "look," including clothes, jewelry, and hairstyle. Why would Peter use this word to describe a woman's look? An element of the word's meaning seems to be "system," "arrangement," or "order." The Bible authors use the term to describe the order of the created globe, the order of humanity in general, the order of humanity postured against God, or the order of a woman's look.

God's Good Creation and Man's Evil Nature

Is God's physical ordered creation bad or good? In Genesis 1 when God said His creation was "very good," He was saying that it perfectly pleased Him, or possibly that it all worked perfectly. His statement is an expression of His satisfaction. When man fell, the creation was *physically* harmed (Gen. 3:17–18; Rom. 8:22), but that harm did not place the physical creation into the category of something *morally* wicked or evil. Of course, God is not satisfied with the present status quo of decay, disease, and death; but the physical creation is still considered to be something delightful and good (1 Tim. 4:4; 6:17; Titus 1:15). Nothing in creation (even meat offered to demons) is morally defiled (see 1 Cor. 10:25–26 in its context). Things in God's creation will not "rub off" on you and make you morally impure in God's sight. God's creation is His (Ps. 24:1) and should not be viewed as evil.

First Timothy 4:4 says, "Every creature [literally 'every creation'] of God is good, and nothing to be refused." The subsequent context indicates that things are good only if they are received with thanksgiving and prayer. This actually substantiates the point that all things are "good." God labels things in creation "good" or "bad" based on the heart of the one using them. "Unto the pure all things are pure: but unto them that are defiled and unbelieving is nothing pure" (Titus 1:15). This verse demonstrates that the location of morality is in the heart of man, not the object man uses. The object used does not actually become evil if someone sins with it (1 Cor. 10:25–26). Rather, the person becomes evil. The heart of man abuses. Things in the earth are in the category of "abused." All this is to say that God considers the creation to be good but victimized by the severe repercussions of man's revolt against God. What ramifications do these facts have for Christians?

Rather than viewing themselves as being defiled by the world, people need to view themselves as the defilers. They are not at risk of *being defiled by* things in the earth; they are at risk of *defiling themselves with* things in the earth. People can escape objects and places, but they can never escape the real problem, which resides within them. Monks in the Middle Ages went to retreatist extremes only to discover in their spartan cells that they could defile anything, even their bread and water. Even their straw mat on which they slept could become an object on which an idolatrous heart fixates itself. Here it is in the common man's nutshell: "It's easy to get the Christian out of the world; it's hard to get the world out of the Christian."

It is very important to fit these facts from Scripture into your worldview. Failing to do so can result in various doctrinal or personal problems. For example, the Pharisees were arrogantly overscrupulous partly because they believed that contact with certain physical objects would automatically defile a person morally. Jesus corrected this faulty presupposition (Mark 7:14–16). Christians today rarely go to the extremes of the Pharisees. However, many Christians who are rightly concerned about personal holiness do have a closely related problem. They view their life as a battle against certain "bad things" and overlook the fact that the Christian life is instead about relating as a sinful being with a holy God. They view things and activities as the enemy and yet can become insensitive to the subtleties of their own deceitful hearts. They may fear or feel animosity toward activities or physical objects when the danger is primarily their own heart. They may unconsciously shift the location of morality to the object— shift responsibility—and resent the "thing" that made them stumble rather than level with their heart and repent of sin. They may define worldliness primarily in terms of contact with objects or involvement in certain activities and miss the multitude of subtle ways their hearts express worldliness. As you read this book on the Internet, realize that the technology itself is not inherently wicked. The issue is what wicked man does with technology. Don't view the computer on your desk as the problem. Don't think of the Internet as a vast "spider web of evil" that should be off limits. Place the problem where it really is— in man's heart and in your heart.

How bad is man's wicked heart? Because man has sinned against God, all men are tainted with a fallen nature, which is incapable of pleasing God (Job 15:16; Rom. 7:18; 8:5–8; Gal. 5:16–21; Eph. 2:3). Every impulse of his heart is sinful (Gen. 6:5). Man is a hardened rebel who is actually described as a hater of God (Rom. 1:30). To make matters worse, man is energized by a powerful demonic being who desires only man's destruction (Eph. 2:1–3).

Furthermore, God holds man completely responsible for every evil deed he commits. Even every word will be judged after death (Matt. 12:36–37; Heb. 9:27). To top it all off, God considers committing a single sin to be a breaking of His whole law (James 2:10) and deserving of hell (Gal. 3:10).

The Earth: A Vast Testing Ground

Since God is so stringent in His standard of judgment and man is fallen and cannot please God, man is in quite a bad predicament. However, God has provided salvation to man through the gracious provision of Christ's death on the cross. And because of this grace, the earth is full both of those who are still estranged from God and of those who are children of God (Matt. 13:38). Those who are truly children of God will continue in faith, overcome "the world" (in the sense of humanity postured against God), and ultimately be delivered from the outpouring of God's wrath on mankind (Heb. 3:14; 1 John 5:4; Rev. 2:11).

The earth viewed from this perspective becomes a very sobering place. It is a vast testing ground in which the children of God are differentiated from the children of the evil one. Life becomes an arena in which God's children are revealed as God brings about through them the works that He has planned all along for them to do (Eph. 2:10; Phil. 2:13). Only at the end of the age are the wheat and tares divided forever (Matt. 13:30). The wheat must spend its whole earthly existence mixed in with the tares.

It is in this kind of world that professing Christian teens live, choose, act, think, and grow up. And God will judge them for how they behave in "all these things" (Eccles. 11:9). Life in God's world is not a game. Life reveals what the eternal destiny will be of every human being. Those who are saved stop continually sinning (1 John 3:9). They no longer abuse the world in which they live (1 Cor. 7:31). But those who are not saved (whether they profess to be or not) do not stop sinning (1 John 3:10). So in a real sense, the children of light and the children of darkness are manifested by how they behave in the world. This is why the New Testament emphasizes personal piety and the moral reformation that occurs in a man's life when he truly accepts Christ (2 Cor. 5:17). Those who are saved are actually able to please God (Rom. 6:1–9), unlike unsaved men (Rom. 8:8; 1 Cor. 2:14). And Christians are responsible to present the members of their bodies in service to God (Rom. 6:10–23). God wants Christians to stop abusing things in the world, to stop using the elements of the world for themselves (2 Cor. 5:15). Those who fail to produce these good works never were God's children to begin with (James 2:14–26; 1 John 2:19).

But even true Christians can be negatively affected by the expressions of sinful men around them. They can (consciously or subconsciously) capitulate to the wrong worldview, can become carnal and wicked (1 Cor. 3:1–3), and thus can lose eternal reward (1 Cor. 3:12–15). Evil communication corrupts good character (1 Cor. 15:33). These Christians can bring upon themselves painful chastisement from God if they continue doing wrong (Heb. 12:5–11), not to mention the heartache and agony they can bring on others around them. Many times faithful pastors all over the world have heard an agonized Christian say, "I know I deserve this punishment for what I did, but I don't know if I can live with the consequences." Such Christians smear the Lord's testimony, ruin their peace of mind, and suffer shaken and guilt-ridden lives, often for years.

The World's Tests

The ideas of fallen people can convince those who profess Christ to live in ways that displease God (Matt. 18:6; 1 Cor. 5:6; 15:33). That is, professing Christians can be tempted to love something else more than they love Christ. Therefore, those who profess Christ must constantly fight a strong seduction to live in ways that displease God. Pleasing God by doing His will is the pivotal issue in a person's existence, for only the one who does God's will can have eternal life (Matt. 7:21; Luke 8:21). Those who profess Christ are in constant danger of loving the world's display of its rebellion against God, and thus they are often warned against doing so in the New Testament (James 4:1–4; 1 John 2:15–17). Such possibilities are what motivated the author of Hebrews to pen the following sobering words:

> Take heed, brethren, lest there be in any of you an evil heart of unbelief, in departing from the living God. But exhort one another daily, while it is called To day; lest any of you be hardened through the deceitfulness of sin. For we are made partakers of Christ, if we hold the beginning of our confidence stedfast unto the end. (Hebrews 3:12–14)

This text does not teach that people can lose their salvation. When a person believes in Christ as his Savior from sin, he is saved forever (John 3:16; Rom. 5:9). Jesus explicitly settled this issue (John 10:28). What Hebrews 3 does teach is that there are those who are attached to the people of God (to Christian congregations or to the Christian subculture) who have made personal reformations in their lives, have conformed to the standards of their personal Christian community, and yet have not believed in Jesus Christ as their Savior from sin. They are unsaved even though they look and act like Christians. These unsaved people are the stony ground in Jesus' parable who receive the good news with joy but have not trusted Christ; therefore, they abandon their superficial attachment to God during times of trial (Matt. 13:20–21).

The world in which we live is a serious place. In a sense, it is the arena in which the great struggle between God and Satan takes place. But the real battlefield between those two foes is the mind and heart of man. How professing Christians respond to the many dangers, trials, and snares in life is the perfect test for manifesting who are God's children and who are not.

The Internet: A Microcosm of the World

Of course, Scripture says much more about the world, but we've considered some of its very important themes. Now let's place the Internet into that world. The Internet is a microcosm of the world—that is, it is a small representative system that holds much of the same opportunities and dangers that the real world does. It's a "mini" world within the real world. A significant difference is that with the Internet almost all the possibilities in the world are within easy reach. When we sit in front of our monitor, we literally have nearly all the possibilities of the vast world no farther away than a few clicks of a mouse. Viewed from the above biblical perspective of the world, the Internet is a spiritually perilous invention. The technology is wonderful and the possibilities for good endless. But because man is an incurable rebel against God, the Internet provides access to some of the worst evils known to man. Just like the world in which we live, the Internet is a stage in which the godly and the ungodly are manifested. God will judge every word we type in e-mail, every website we choose, every purchase, every decision we make on the Internet. Every moment in life is recorded in the omniscient mind of God, and every one of our actions, including what we do on the Internet, will be judged by Him. There are no insignificant moments. Those who reject God's ways and choose to use the Internet for what God hates will never be able to escape the Almighty. God always brings His enemies to justice and always chastens His wayward children.

What we are really saying is that there are more temptations available than ever before because of the Internet. The passages that we need to search for are ones that deal with the very serious issue of temptation. Those who struggle with Internet pornography, shameful chatrooms, online gambling, uncontrolled debt, plagiarized online sources, stolen copyrighted materials, or any other vice made accessible by the Internet will find Essay 2, "Temptation," to be helpful in their fight against sin. The ultimate question, however, in any fight against sin is whether you really want freedom or not. If you do want power over sin, it is available to those who are saved through the power of God's indwelling Spirit and God's Word (Ps. 119:11; Gal. 5:16).

TEMPTATION

by Thomas Parr

As we have demonstrated, any passage in the Bible about temptation and the Christian's proper relationship to the world is relevant to this discussion. But the Internet has its own qualities that suggest that we ought to be even more specific. First, the Internet provides seeming *privacy*. People who sin on the Internet try to do so in secret, due to the inherent privacy of personal computers. Second, the Internet provides an amazing amount of *accessibility*. Someone with access to the web could probably go on forever finding new sites at which to feed carnal desire. What passage in the Bible matches well with such a situation? One particular passage comes to mind.

David's Temptation (2 Samuel 11)

Background

So far we have striven to *understand the modern situation* and have demonstrated that passages on temptation *legitimately apply* to this modern situation. Now we must *consider the historical background and context of the passage* that we have decided is most appropriate to study and *let the Bible direct its own applications*, using other passages to bolster the argument.

David experienced God's blessing in an ever-increasing way. He was a lowly shepherd who lived with the sheep (1 Sam. 16:11; 2 Sam. 7:8) and was exalted and anointed king of Israel (1 Sam. 16:13). For most of his life he enjoyed consistent military success (1 Sam. 17:48–50; 18:6–7; 2 Sam. 5:17–25). Though he lived for many years as a fugitive from Saul, he was protected by God (1 Sam. 19:18–24; 23:14, 26–28) and saw his enemies gradually abased until he was finally established as king over Judah and Israel (2 Sam. 2:4; 5:3).

The years that David spent in the wilderness fleeing from Saul were full of hardship for David. He lived in caves (1 Sam. 22:1). Harassed by the maniacal king Saul, he lost faith and fled to pagans for protection (1 Sam. 27:1). He had all his possessions and family stolen by invaders and was nearly murdered by his followers (1 Sam. 30:1–6). He escaped from his enemies by the slightest margin (1 Sam. 23:26–28). He was beleaguered by constant attempts on his life (1 Sam. 23:14). Though God always delivered him, his life was nevertheless very difficult.

Once he gained the throne of Judah, David began to experience nearly unprecedented success. He gained victory over his rivals in Israel (2 Sam. 3:27; 4:8) and yet maintained a good reputation in the eyes of Israel (2 Sam. 3:36). He defeated various enemy countries (2 Sam. 5:17–25; 8:1–14; 10:6–19) and reestablished the proper worship of Jehovah in Israel (2 Sam. 6:15–18; 1 Chron. 15:12–15, 25–29). He received from God the promise that his line would never be rejected as Saul's was (2 Sam. 7:13–16). God gave David rest from all of his enemies and made him a mighty hero in the earth (2 Sam. 7:1, 9). David enjoyed more success than nearly anyone in the ancient world.

But with such success comes the temptation to abuse it. David had the adulation of his people, the submission of all his enemies, the stability of his nation, and the power and prerogatives that accompany being one of the most successful monarchs in history. He had control over his time, control over his environment, and opportunity for unlimited privacy and pleasures. As a fallen human being with the world within reach, David faced many temptations to rebel against God.

Unfortunately, David disobeyed God on numerous occasions before he ever became successful, so disobedience had become a pattern that he sometimes fell into. When Saul's hatred of him had shown itself to be irreversible, David, in desperation, resorted to lies and deceit in order to protect himself (1 Sam. 20:6; 21:2). He fled to pagan nations for help (1 Sam. 21:11–15; 22:3–4) until God commanded him to return to Judah (22:5); but afterwards, he disobeyed out of fear and returned to the Philistines (1 Sam. 25:1; 27:1). David began to manifest problems in his sexual life. He began to take multiple wives (1 Sam. 25:42–43; 2 Sam. 3:2–5), something the Law expressly forbids (Deut. 17:17). So early on, David is characterized as someone who is sexually deviant as well as a deceitful manipulator. When a person like this is given unlimited power and access to whatever pleasures he desires, the result will be what is revealed in 2 Samuel 11. David chose to rebel against God rather than serve Him, and he paid for it the rest of his life.

David's Fall and Its Consequences

Verse one of 2 Samuel 11 begins by telling us that rather than going out to war when kings traditionally did, David stayed back in the comfort of the royal palace and sent his treacherous sidekick Joab to fight his battles for him. What did David do in those early spring days? Verse two implies that he indulged his desire for ease. At evening he arose from his bed and went to the roof of his royal house. From the vantage point of the roof, he spotted an attractive woman. At this point David was tempted in a way that many today are tempted. David was a man who was used to indulging his sensual desires. His position in the world allowed him to get away with it. But in 2 Samuel 11:3 we see David tempted in a way in which he had never been. He was tempted to commit adultery—to not only sin with another woman, but in so doing to cause her to betray her covenant with her husband. David, unused to denying himself, gave in to the temptation and committed adultery.

But David's sin did not stop there. As sin often does, it took him farther than he thought it would go. Bathsheba was carrying David's child. The next few verses tell in horrific detail David's desperate lies, his manipulative deceit, and his eventual murder of Bathsheba's husband, Uriah the Hittite, a man who was one of his loyal mighty men (2 Sam. 23:8, 39). Second Samuel 12:10–11 tells us that even though David genuinely repented, God solemnly promised to chasten David by giving him trouble the rest of his days. David could not escape the consequences of his sin. His life then took a tragic downturn as God worked out those consequences. David's son by Bathsheba died (2 Sam. 12:19). His son Amnon raped his daughter Tamar (2 Sam. 13:1–14). Tamar's brother Absalom murdered Amnon and tried to usurp the throne from David (2 Sam. 13:22–33; 15:1–12). With great sorrow, David had to flee Jerusalem and his palace (2 Sam. 15:13–30). Providentially, the takeover failed, and Absalom was killed by David's henchman Joab (2 Sam. 18:1–17). David's heart was broken over the death of Absalom, a son whom he greatly loved (2 Sam. 18:33).

The story of David is a tragedy, as God exalts a humble servant and then must humble him for his pride and rebellion. What salvages David's life is God's promise that He would never take His favor away from David (2 Sam. 7:14–15); and David repented of his sin, trusted God, was saved, and showed evidence of the Holy Spirit's working. David was no more deserving of blessing than Saul. But God had promised to eternally bless David. David recognized he was not worthy of such favor (2 Sam. 7:18–21), and he hoped in it to the end of his life (2 Sam. 23:5).

Universal Principles

Now let's apply David's story to our lives in at least four ways.

First, if we tolerate sin in our lives, we allow ourselves to become vulnerable to greater sins. The important battles are fought *before* the big temptation arrives. How we fight the smaller battles determines how we will handle the larger ones. We should never tolerate in our lives even the slightest amount of what God hates.

Second, situations of ease and availability present more temptations. The more power or opportunities we have, the more ways our sinful nature can express itself. In our society the common man has almost as much power over his personal time and environment as David had as a successful ancient king. We therefore, as fallen humans, have unprecedented temptations before us. We have vast opportunity and great evil within our grasp. Who we are on the inside will come out in our actions. And who we are on the inside determines our eternal future. Only the power of the Holy Spirit, received by faith in Christ's atonement, will enable us to overcome the many dangers, toils, and snares that await us.

Third, God punishes sin, even in His children. He will never let His children get away with rebellion. Those who are saved and indwelt by the Spirit, and yet who choose to embrace the world, subject themselves to God's often very painful chastening.

Fourth, even though God's children are punished for their sin, they can always rest in the fact that God will never leave or forsake them (Heb. 13:5–6). The only hope for David was God's promise of an eternal covenant. David had no righteousness of his own that could guarantee God's favor. He simply had God's promise that "my faithfulness and my mercy shall be with him. . . . My mercy will I keep for him for evermore" (Ps. 89:24, 28). Christians have promises that are just as sure. "For all the promises of God . . . are yea, and . . . Amen" to those who are in Christ (2 Cor. 1:20). We can be confident that if God has started working in our lives, He will not leave us as an unfinished product (Phil. 1:6). We can be confident that God will energize in us the willingness and the ability to do His will (Phil. 2:13). We can be confident that God will grant us forgiveness every time we ask for it (1 John 1:9). We can know that "the blood of Jesus Christ his Son cleanseth [Greek: continually, or keeps on, cleansing] us from all sin" (1 John 1:7).

One of the greatest New Testament promises that Christians are entitled to enjoy is found in Hebrews 4:14–16.

Seeing then that [since then] *we have a great high priest* [the Hebrew official in charge of representing the people to God. Without a priest, there was no relationship between God and fallen man], *that is passed into the heavens* [our high priest is not an earthly priest. He has gone to heaven and represents us there eternally. Thus we have eternal access to God, never to be hindered or interrupted], *Jesus the Son of God* [this high priest is not a mere man; He is the Son of God. God Himself represents us to Himself], *let us hold fast our profession. For we have not an high priest which cannot be touched with the feeling of our infirmities* [Jesus, who was also a man, can totally understand and sympathize with all our weaknesses. We do not approach an unfeeling tyrant but rather a tenderhearted brother who loves us more than we can know]; *but was in all points tempted like as we are, yet without sin* [Jesus was sinless but experienced the full power of temptation, something none of us will ever know. Jesus understands sin's deceptiveness and pull more than anyone]. *Let us therefore come boldly unto the throne of grace, that we may obtain mercy* [compassion], *and find grace* [unmerited favor] *to help in* [any] *time of need.*

Christians have a position of indescribable privilege with God. "He that spared not his own Son, but delivered him up for us all, how shall he not with him also freely give us all things?" (Rom. 8:32). Certainly, victory over sin is one of the things He will freely give us. "If we ask any thing according to his will, he heareth us" (1 John 5:14). Let us therefore prove our standing with God (2 Pet. 1:10) and triumph over this sinful world. If we are His, we *will* triumph. We must "believe only" (Luke 8:50). Faith is what overcomes the world (1 John 5:4). And if the demons of fear and desire do not relent, the only option is to flee to Christ and say with Peter and Jacob, "Lord, to whom shall we go? thou hast the words of eternal life" (John 6:68) and "I will not let thee go, except thou bless me" (Gen. 32:26). Those who come to Christ this way will never be cast out (John 6:37).

Never fall into the trap of thinking victory and growth come without a face-to-face relationship with Jesus Christ. A relationship with God is more than sitting alone in a room reading a Bible. Many people have studied the Bible for their whole lives but have never come to know its Author. Your relationship with God must be a melding of two minds: yours and Christ's. It must be two people relating:

one the master, the other the servant. It must be personal and fulfilling. This relationship demands faith acting in prayer—cries, laments, exultations, petitions, and every other kind of interaction the Psalms show to be appropriate in relating to God. Having this interaction with God is what it means to know God experientially. No victory will come without it. Victory never comes except in vital, living communion with God in Christ.

We fail because we do not love God enough. If we truly loved the Lord Jesus the way He deserves, no temptation could ever seem appealing. But because our hearts are cold toward Him, our desires roam to other (idolatrous) loves. We must learn to fully appreciate, enjoy, and take advantage of our New Testament privileges. Many Christians don't even realize they have distinct privileges in being related to Christ. They are like beggars who have been given a billion dollars but don't have any way of being able to grasp the magnitude of such a gift. So they continue to sit in the filth and beg. The new birth brings great honor; we are now born into God's family and can cry, "Abba, Father" (Rom. 8:15). Only when we come to understand these truths will the spirit of thankfulness and joy echo in our hearts and overflow in a life of victory that is pleasing to God.

CHRISTIANS AND CULTURE

by Thomas Parr

I don't know what you think of when you hear the word *culture*. Maybe you think of films, music, and Picasso. Perhaps you think of opera and the fat lady singing. Whatever particular aspects of culture come to mind when you hear that word, culture actually consists of much more. It refers to the totality of human endeavor and thought in a people group. Most people have not evaluated their culture in any rational or biblical way. To them, their culture is the ways things are, and they simply live in it. But culture is much too important to treat so casually, especially in recent days when it has so dramatically changed for the worse.

> It might seem an extreme assertion at first, but I believe that the challenge of living with popular culture may well be as serious for modern Christians as persecution and plagues were for the saints of earlier centuries. Being thrown to the lions or living in the shadow of gruesome death are fairly straightforward if unattractive threats. Enemies that come loudly and visibly are usually much easier to fight than those that are undetectable. Physical affliction (even to the point of death) for the sake of Christ is a heavy cross, but at least it can be readily recognized at the time as a trial of faith. But the erosion of character, the spoiling of innocent pleasures, and the cheapening of life itself that often accompany modern popular culture can occur so subtly that we believe nothing has happened.[1]

Since the Internet is a microcosm of the world (see Essay 1), a book on the Internet should help us understand human culture in general and the Christian's proper relationship to it. There are many hotly debated opinions on this issue among Christians today. Some Christian leaders tell us that culture in whatever form it appears is good and is even an expression of Christ. Other Christian leaders take a semi-monastic view: try to get yourself as disconnected from our culture as possible because it is evil (see Essay 4 for a more detailed discussion of various views). Of course, our desire should be to understand what the Bible teaches about culture and the proper relation to its various forms. As we have seen elsewhere in this book (see Essay 1), the Bible is intended by God to give us direction for every issue we may face in life. The Bible is a sufficient moral compass to guide us wherever we find ourselves. Therefore, it is not unnatural to ask, What does the Bible tell us about culture? Though the word *culture* does not appear in the Bible, we know from 2 Timothy 3:16 that the Bible gives us principles that inform us about it.

Culture and Its Origins

What is the essence of culture? What qualities make it what it is? *First*, culture is universally experienced by all people groups. Regardless of its state of development, every people group creates culture of one kind or another. So it is very likely that cultural capacity is something that God instilled into man as part of man's partaking of the image of God. Man is a social being much as God is a social being. God has enjoyed fellowship among the persons of the Trinity from all eternity. Man's relationship to his environment and to other men and the form that relationship takes reflect man's unique role as image-bearer. Culture making is a mark of being human, much like man's ability to form complex language and to reflect on himself.

Second, men have often analyzed what they, by their God-given nature, produce. Multiple sources on this issue indicate that the following aspects of culture are widely observed among men:

1. The word *culture* is used to represent the totality of the thought and endeavor of a people group.[2]

2. The word *culture* is used to refer to the various customs (e.g., the common language; typical clothing types and fashions, including materials commonly used; and prevalent events such as religious events, sporting events, or other public displays) of people groups and the diverse ways customs are practiced.

3. The word *culture* is used to refer to more general segments of the culture-at-large, such as music, art, literature, drama, industry, manufacturing, religion, philosophy, economics, etc. [3]

4. Culture itself is values-laden. That is, the individual aspects of culture (music, art, etc.) are expressed in accordance with the human authors' viewpoints about ethics, morals, truth, etc.[4]

5. Culture can be divided into at least three sub-categories. High culture assumes transcendent moral values and focuses on

preserving the great achievements of the past. Folk culture assumes transcendent moral values and focuses on preserving the thought-forms of a particular community or sub-culture. Popular culture (a relatively new phenomenon) isn't concerned with transcendent values but makes mass, popular opinion and fickle preference its greatest values, and it focuses on profit-making and constant novelty.[5] In modern America, popular culture has largely consumed the other two subcategories of culture. Now, even elements of high culture are either praised or ignored by the cultural mouthpieces (the media) on the basis of their profitability and popular reception.

Third, Scripture also refers to this phenomenon that men have termed *culture*, even giving us clues to its origin in the story of the creation of man. Our discussion here will support what we said earlier about our capacity for culture being an essential part of being human. Don't skip the following discussion, which is the foundation for the conclusions we will come to. Without it we cannot justify any observations about culture.

Genesis 1 typically is used to prove that the universe was made in six literal days, and of course the passage teaches this. However, the passage also teaches a number of other foundational truths, one being God's first command to His newly created vice regent—man. Genesis 1:26–28 includes the first record of God's intention for man. First, man was made in God's image. This means that man has certain characteristics that are like some of God's attributes. Man can reason, reflect, speak, and make moral judgments—activities the rest of the physical creation cannot do. Second, man was to have dominion over the earth. Many people have tried to make this verse apply only to such activities as fishing, hunting, and animal training. But the verses go beyond this. They tell man to have dominion "over all the earth" and to "subdue it." The theme of man's dominion repeatedly recurs in the subsequent context, helping to define what subduing the earth involves.

Genesis 2:5 comments that at this point in God's creative process, there were land and seed (resources), but there was no "man to till the ground" (harnessing the resources, i.e., "subduing"). This implies that one of man's purposes was to cultivate the earth, an activity that has not ceased since the creation of man. This assumption is confirmed in Genesis 2:15, which relates that God placed Adam in the garden so that Adam would work and preserve the land. Adam was free to eat of all the trees except one. God placed one restriction on His vice regent so that there would be a standard by which man's submission and loyalty to God could be judged. Man was to rule, but he was to rule under the rule of God. Genesis 2:19 relates that God allowed Adam to name the animals He had created. Here we see man, endowed with the power of reason, using his innate ability under the authority of God. This is a glimpse of the image of God working in proper submission to his Creator. So we see that man's cultivation of the ground and his naming of the animals were part of his dominion as vice regent under his sovereign Creator. The theme of man's dominion continues like a thread through the next few chapters.

In Chapter 3 we observe man's failure to maintain his proper submission to God. Man revolts against his Sovereign, the God to whom the stars and planets render immediate and continual obedience. The rest of Scripture chronicles the result of man's sin and God's response to it in judgment and redemption. Man's sin had a direct effect on the command of dominion. No longer would the ground cooperate with man; it would bring forth thorns (3:18). No longer would man find dominion to be thoroughly enjoyable; it would now become an arduous and often sorrowful experience (3:17–19).

Though man had sinned, he nevertheless continued to explore possible ways to have dominion over the earth. Man's constitution in the image of God provided nearly limitless ways for interacting with the world around him and subduing it to his will. But now that sin had entered the world, man's dominion became perverted. The chapters that follow present man not only discovering new avenues of dominion but also failing to use them for God's honor. Chapter 4 records the story of Cain and Abel. Both fulfilled the dominion command in their respective occupations (farmer, shepherd), but Cain tried to approach God in a way that God had not prescribed. When Cain was rebuked and warned, he showed the depths of the sinful nature by murdering his brother. So we see dominion perverted. Genesis 4:17–22 details various constructive ways men began to harness the resources God had put at their disposal. Cain's son Enoch built a city. Jabal, one of Cain's descendants, started the practice of dwelling in tents and tending livestock. Jubal discovered a new way to enhance his surroundings. He used plant life (most likely gourds or possibly wood) to form instruments that would produce enjoyable sounds. He was father of those who play musical instruments; thus the arts were born. Tubal-cain became the first forger, making various tools from bronze and iron.

Chapter 5, known as the "death chapter" for its genealogies punctuated by the phrase "and he died," emphasizes another aspect of existence after the Fall—loss of eternal life (cf. 3:22–24). Chapter 6 emphasizes an additional way that men put their dominion ability to use: they killed each other. God's main reason for bringing the Flood was that violence filled the earth. Sinful men had multiplied on the earth and had found new ways to subdue it. But they did not make just eating utensils and tent pegs. They made swords and spears—instruments for killing men. Men had become obstacles to one another. As we have seen in Cain's case, it didn't take sinful men long to figure out what they could do about such obstacles. Men cast off the restraints of conscience and no longer used their power of dominion for the honor of God but for their own ends. Man placed himself at the center of his universe, and by and large the world was filled with people who didn't concern themselves with God at all. This wasn't just the case in Noah's time. After the Flood, one of the most significant displays of man's self-worship is the event that is related in the story of Babel in Genesis 11. "The elements of the [Babel] story are timelessly characteristic of the spirit of the world."[6]

The rest of God's creation continued to serve His every command just as it had when the stars sprung into existence at His Word. But now mankind had corrupted its way upon the earth so that men forgot God and "changed the glory of the uncorruptible God into an image made like to corruptible man" and "served the creature more than the Creator" (Rom. 1:23, 25). Men united in their efforts to exalt man and exclude God, which is seen in their humanistic statements in Genesis 11:4: "Go to, let us build us a city and a tower, whose top may reach unto heaven; and let us make us a name, lest we be scattered abroad upon the face of the whole earth." This statement is significant for a number of reasons.

First, the statement "whose top may reach unto heaven" (more literally translated "its top in the heavens") clearly evidences human pride of accomplishment. This essentially means that man had come to take a self-centered pride in his abilities. Hence, the pursuit of excellence became a man-centered goal. God was not thanked as the giver of all gifts (1 Cor. 4:7; James 1:17). Man exalted himself as autonomous. Many commentators think that this attempt to build the tower reflects man's religious attempt to either autonomously approach his own concept of deity or to deify himself.[7] This proposal seems to find support from the archaeological evidence of the time. The ziggurats of ancient Babylon contained temples to heathen gods at their pinnacles.

Second, the statement "let us make us a name" (better translated "let us make a name for ourselves") tells us the purpose for their endeavor: the glory of man. Though man is God's (Ps. 24:1), man wants God to have nothing to do with him. Rather, he wants to replace God with an image "like to corruptible man" (Rom. 1:23). Giving God glory is the farthest thing from his mind. Thus man becomes totally secular. In his mind, his existence and interaction with the creation have nothing to do with God. Man, the vice regent, has thrown off God's sovereign rule. Man is left to find meaning in only his surroundings.

Third, the statement "lest we be scattered abroad upon the face of the whole earth" shows again the pride of man, though that may be hard to see on the surface. In a fallen world, man often faces life-threatening dangers. At the very least, he faces the constant threat of personal loss. In the ancient world in which dispersal went along with tribal warfare, gathering as many people together in a city and inducing the populace to an almost nationalistic zeal for themselves would serve to build a sense of security. How does this display pride? Babel put collective humanity in the place of God. God says, "Cursed be the man that trusteth in man, and maketh flesh his arm" (Jer. 17:5). But blessed is the man whose confidence is in God (Jer. 17:7). God is the true mighty one upon whom we must always trust. Failure to trust God is the ultimate insult to Him. It is essentially rejecting Him and saying, "No thanks, I can handle it on my own." What those in Babel did was another manifestation of their secular humanistic mindset.

At this point we should draw some conclusions from this biblical evidence. *First*, we can see that culture making is the direct result of the command that God gave man to have dominion over the earth. Man was to utilize the various resources that were at his disposal in the earth. And so we see man utilizing fruit for food, skins for clothes (3:21), the ground for crops, clay for bricks for houses, hides for tents, gourds for musical instruments, and metals for tools and weapons. When we look around at our environment, we see evidence that man is still carrying out this command. Desks and bookshelves are made from wood or metal, shoes from leather and rubber, computers from plastics, metals, and other elements. Man has been given an amazing ability to control his environment and put it into service for himself. But, *second*, because man is a fallen being, he strives to find meaning and security in himself or in other people rather than God. Man becomes "all in all" for man. The result, inevitably, is a culture that is secular, in which autonomous man—his desires, preferences, passions, and values—determines what is considered good and beautiful. Man's endeavors are divorced from any meaning beyond serving man's safety, pleasure, and convenience. Anything that restricts man's freedom to pursue what makes him happy is the greatest threat. Psalm 2:1–3 expresses this spirit of the world in graphic terms:

> Why do the heathen rage, and the people imagine a vain thing? The kings of the earth set themselves, and the rulers take counsel together, against the Lord, and against his anointed, saying, Let us break their bands asunder, and cast away their cords from us.

The apostle Paul explained the only logical conclusion to rejecting God and living for this life only: "What advantageth it me, if the dead rise not? let us eat and drink; for to morrow we die" (1 Cor. 15:32). In other words, in a materialistic worldview (a worldview that decides to leave God out and assert that only matter exists), personal well-being and pleasure are the highest values, and they will drive a culture.

So what is the Christian to do in today's society? The most helpful observation in answering this question is that culture is the expression of a group's various worldviews. A people group's activities and how those people practice them (i.e., their culture) is the result of the various worldviews finding expression among them. The worldview that has the greatest hearing will have the greatest dominance in that culture and will profoundly affect cultural expression.

Relating to Human Culture

Learn to Discern

Since men create culture, and men are by nature value-laden, culture is inevitably an expression of a worldview. Therefore, a culture's goodness or badness should be determined by comparing the culture with the standard—God's Word. Cultural expressions (words, sounds, activities) that are antagonistic to God should be classified as what the Bible calls "the world." But how do we know when something is antagonistic to God?

Words are antagonistic to God when they contradict His truth. Friedrich Nietzsche's classic statement that "God is dead" meant that modern man has found the concept of God no longer useful. This idea obviously contradicts God's Word. But antagonism to God is not limited to explicit statements such as Nietzsche's. Antagonism to God is most often expressed in subtly implicit ways. These implicit ways are often more persuasive than outright statements because, instead of engaging people's intellect, they subtly solicit people to absorb the underlying value based solely on the emotion of the moment. For example, when someone curses, he is saying much more than the meaning of the foul word that he spoke. He's claiming that it is morally acceptable to say what he just said. Each time such things occur (whether in actual experience, in print, or on screen), the implicit value judgments underlying them are taught (and are subsequently "caught" by those who are not committed to an absolute value beyond themselves). Another example could be this quotation: "Life is short, so live fast and die hard." Many people cannot discern the implicit theological assertions in this statement. It assumes a materialistic universe (one in which only matter exists) and offhandedly rejects the idea of impending judgment by an offended deity. In other words, it is completely antagonistic to the Christian worldview. How about this well-known quotation: "He who dies with the most toys wins"? This statement assumes that life is a game in which people are competing and that the way to win the game is to accumulate as much "stuff" as possible. The first quotation assumes that "living fast" (i.e., engaging in a lifestyle that includes illicit sex, drugs, or alcohol) is the way to enjoy a short existence. The second quotation assumes that acquiring many material possessions is the way to enjoy life. But both quotations assume a materialistic universe in which a person exists for only a few decades. Thus both are antagonistic to the Christian worldview, which asserts that all men will exist forever in one of two places: a place of eternal happiness or a place of eternal torment. In the worldview of the two quotations, all that matters is now. There is no transcendent meaning. In the Christian worldview every moment is meaningful forever, because everyone will be judged for every detail of his life, even every stray word that he speaks (Matt. 12:36).

Let's consider someone who spends a lot of his time trying to entertain himself by watching TV. He may not realize it, but he is saying something about eternal matters. He is saying there is nothing more important than his entertainment. This is a statement about the ultimate—essentially that there is no absolute truth bigger than himself that deserves his time and attention. Nothing is more important than his personal well-being and pleasure. But is this really true? Is there no greater purpose for our existence than our own enjoyment? If there is no greater purpose, then it truly is wise to "eat, drink, and be merry, for tomorrow we die." However, anyone who tries to live this way will soon discover that he quickly grows weary of the enjoyments that he once delighted in (Eccles. 1–2). He will move aimlessly from pleasure to pleasure to satisfy his desires but will find himself always moving on to something new, never satisfied. Leaving a path littered with the husks of discarded loves, he will always wander aimlessly ahead, searching for something new to consume. This is the case because man can be fully satisfied only when he finds that the purpose for his existence is in God. As St. Augustine said so eloquently, "Thou hast formed us for Thyself, and our hearts are restless till they find rest in Thee."[8]

But not only words implicitly teach a worldview. All expressions of the human soul do so. Works of art, musical arrangements, non-verbal actions—all teach a certain moral perspective. We can all think of a work of art, body language, or musical arrangement that carries subtle (or not-so-subtle) values. The very sight or sound of them creates a certain mental atmosphere that God says is not proper for people to have, and thus these nonverbal expressions are antagonistic to God. Many today argue that musical arrangements are neutral and that any particular sound is culturally determined—that is, a certain sound may mean one thing in one culture and something completely different in another. While no doubt this is true to some extent, there are certain sounds that communicate the same message to any culture because they are expressions of the foundational qualities of the human soul. For example, a battle song will tend not to sound like easy-listening music, and people will probably never calm down to the loud crash of a dozen trash cans falling. The story in the Old Testament of Moses coming down from Mount Sinai helps make the point that there are certain sounds that communicate the same values to all cultures. What is the sound of self-abandonment and lack of self-control like? When Moses and Joshua were descending the Mount, Joshua heard music that was being played in the camp below where the Israelites were engaging in riotous idolatry. But when Joshua heard the music, he mistook it for the crashes and cries of battle. Moses corrected him and said it was "the noise of them that sing do I hear" (Exod. 32:18). The people in the camp had abandoned God and cast off all restraint, and the music that accompanied their indulgence was in keeping with it. Their music went right along with their casting off self-control, something that is antithetical to a Spirit-filled life (Gal. 5:23). Any cultural expression that transgresses the bounds of what God prescribes for human behavior is antagonistic to God. God commands Christians to "keep [guard] thy heart" (Prov. 4:23) and to "have no fellowship with [don't share in] the unfruitful works of darkness, but rather reprove them" (Eph. 5:11). God's heart is grieved when so many of His people set themselves up in antagonism to Himself by aligning themselves with the expressions of sinful men (James 4:4).

The objective in our encounters with culture is to come away from those encounters loving God more than we did before. This demands that we learn to discern between what is good and evil in culture. But we must not simply discern between them; we must "abhor that which is evil; cleave to that which is good" (Rom. 12:9). We have not re-mained loyal to God until we have the proper emotional response to the good and bad in culture.

"The world" in culture can often be very difficult to discern. This is especially so with the Internet. Often man's fallen presuppositions have infiltrated the very structure of the technology. For an in-depth discussion of the subtle problems of the Internet, see Essay 5.

Avoid Isolation as well as Worldliness

Since our culture is so inundated with secularism and hedonism, should we have as little to do with it as possible? Many concerned Christians have been greatly disturbed by the trends in our culture and have opted for a very detached lifestyle. They avoid the very conventions of our particular culture; that is, they reject music not played by Christians, they won't listen to a radio station not run by Christians, they ignore most films, they won't go to shopping malls, and they generally carry around with them a suspicion of American culture. They would rather have films and plays be turned into preaching services, and they are ambivalent toward anything that doesn't feel like church. While no doubt we should retain a healthy suspicion of a culture dominated by "the world," this extreme detach-ment can nevertheless be very detrimental to the cause of Christ.

Christians who are constantly suspicious and unaware of the preva-lent thought forms in our culture can obstruct people's entering the Kingdom, something Christ condemned (Matt. 23:13). For example, often those who take this retreatist view will limit their reading options to books that were written in previous time periods, because they con-sider the modern venues so full of trash. (True, reading classic litera-ture and avoiding unsuitable modern works are important.) However, Christians who cut themselves off from our culture to this extreme are mistaken because they become familiar with the thought forms of an-other age but are aliens to those of the modern age. They learn much that is valuable, but are strangers in their own time. Consequently, they are unable to relate to the common man. The common man is awash in our culture, has no maturity, and cannot discern. To him, such a Christian is an enigma with whom he has no cultural common ground. Such Christians cut off blessings to the common man by retreating from our culture. We must have the wisdom to be able to see what is mandated biblically and what is simply cultural preference.

Cultural preferences must be rejected whenever they obstruct the "weightier matter" of love for people. Our attitude toward cultural matters must be like Paul's. He willingly laid down his cultural preferences in order to win people to Jesus Christ (1 Cor. 9:22–23). Of course, Paul wouldn't lay down a *biblical command* for the sake of winning people to Christ. No, he felt strongly that "it is never right to do wrong in order to get a chance to do right."[9] But whenever a *cultural preference* became an obstacle to people's reception of him, Paul would lay it down. We must do the same. Paul's viewpoint did not allow dabbling in whatever cultural expression he desired so that his life became an indolent joy ride. No, Paul was talking about sacrificing cultural preferences for Christ's cause, not personal pleasure. We must hold our cultural preferences with loose hands, willing to sacrifice them for Christ. And if our cultural preference is detachment, we must lay that aside, because detachment from our culture forces people to live without salt and light.

Failure to interact with culture also shuts off Christians from opportunities to discern good from bad in our culture. Often the Christian who is least familiar with our culture is also the Christian who cannot discern. He has made for himself a cocoon, a Christian subculture that functions very much like the TV and the couch do for the worldly man. He stays in his comfortable environment and never experiences the jarring clash of worldviews that promotes critical thinking and cements biblical conviction. Often, along with this comes a spoon-fed attitude that accepts teaching without vigorously comparing it to the Bible. This results in flabby Christians who are increasingly estranged from God's Word. Of course, a person who immerses himself in culture can end up at the opposite extreme, tacitly condoning or even embracing the bad in culture. Either extreme is wrong. We must interact with culture, discriminating between the good and the bad and abhorring what is evil (Rom. 12:9). This exercising of our faculties to discern good from evil (Heb. 5:14) will also allow us to meet the common man where he is and help him learn to subject all things to Christ (2 Cor. 10:5).

Failing to interact to some extent with culture can also lead to self-deception. Many of those who distance themselves begin to view worldliness as doing particular things they won't do. But worldliness occurs whenever the heart fixates upon something on earth and is willing to sin against God for it. This is true worldliness. And a person who won't view films or visit malls can be more worldly than those who do. For example, a person who reads theological classics can covet them, actually forget God because of them, and read them instead of his Bible. Worldliness manifests itself in many forms, and often those who define it narrowly are guilty of it in areas they can't see.

Interacting with culture can be a very enriching experience. But we must never forget that our heart is deceptive and can easily grow cold towards God. We must be ever vigilant to guard our heart to ensure that the Lord is king there (Prov. 4:23). Failure to be on guard constantly is the first sign of spiritual decline, because it shows we are not taking God seriously when He says our heart is deceitful and we must always guard it. We must also search the Scriptures to conclude definitively what is inappropriate for Christians to experience. Otherwise, involvement in culture will turn into worldliness. Finally, we must remember that the primary reasons we relate to culture are to know and love God and His world better, to discern "the world" in culture from God's truth in culture, and to relate to our fellow men, most of whom are alienated from the God they were created to glorify.

---

[1]Kenneth A. Myers, *All God's Children and Blue Suede Shoes: Christians and Popular Culture* (Wheaton, IL: Crossway, 1989), xiii–xiv.

[2]*The American Heritage College Dictionary*, 4th ed., s.v. "Culture"; Myers, 27; H. Richard Niebuhr, *Christ and Culture* (New York: Harper & Row, 1951. Expanded fiftieth anniversary ed., San Francisco: HarperSanFrancisco, 2001), 32.

[3]Points 2 and 3 can be substantiated from the following: Myers, 34; *Encyclopedia Britannica*, 15th ed., s.v. "Culture"; Niebuhr, 32.

[4]T. S. Eliot, "Notes Towards the Definition of Culture," in *Christianity and Culture* (New York: Harcourt Brace & Company, 1976), 100; *Encyclopedia Britannica*, 15th ed., s.v. "Culture"; Henry R. Van Til, *The Calvinistic Concept of Culture* (Grand Rapids, MI: Baker, 1959, 1972), 157.

[5]The comments on the different kinds of culture are based on Myers, 53–73.

[6]Derek Kidner, *Genesis: An Introduction and Commentary* (Downer's Grove, IL: Inter-Varsity Press, 1968), 109.

[7]Bruce Waltke, *Genesis: A Commentary* (Grand Rapids, MI: Zondervan, 2001), 179; Gordon Wenham, *Genesis 1-15* (Nashville: Thomas Nelson, 1987), 239; Matthew Henry, *Commentary on Genesis* (Peabody, MA: Hendrickson Publishers, Incorporated, 1991).

[8]Augustine, *Confessions*, trans. J. G. Pilkington (Oxford: Oxford University Press, 1998), 1.1.

[9]*Chapel Sayings of Dr. Bob Jones Sr.* (Greenville, SC: Bob Jones University, n.d.), 10; based on Romans 3:8.

OUR QUEST FOR CONSISTENCY

by Michael Osborne

If you drive through the rolling farmland of Lancaster County, Pennsylvania, you have to watch out for Amish buggies sharing the road. Horses clip clop aloofly along as if it's natural to share the road with tractor trailers going forty-five miles per hour. Also in Lancaster County, you can find numerous Christian retailers, many of which sell Christian heavy-metal CDs, T-shirts incorporating Jesus' name into popular advertising slogans, and purportedly Christian self-help books resembling the humanism-saturated *Chicken Soup for the Soul* series. What contrast! Truly, religious responses to culture vary widely.

If you interact with Christian youth, you're probably aware of the many issues that face you. What should determine your music listening habits? Are there particular magazines that are "over the line"? What clothing and jewelry should men and women wear, and in what situations? What about patronizing restaurants that serve alcohol? Is movie attendance ever OK? If yes, what would make movie attendance OK? Delving into more details, what about renting videos? Which videos could you rent? Do ratings automatically qualify or disqualify films for viewing? How do we sort all these questions? Truly, questions about Christians and culture are legion.

So many questions, so many responses. Even within my small Christian high school years ago, a mad scientist's mix of volatile opinions was ready to blow whenever catalyzed by the right question. And so we'd fall to debating. Looking back on those upstart theologians—myself included—I'm tempted to sarcasm like Job's: "No doubt but ye are the people, and wisdom shall die with you" (12:2). But if the specters of the past were to demand answers from me now, I'd have to admit sheepishly that I don't have definitive answers. But my post–high-school experience has not been in vain. In addition to knocking the wind out of my rhetoric (mostly—rumor has it I'm still sinful), college and seminary training and work for BJU Press have not fed me answers but rather shaped *how* I think. Perhaps the best help I could offer to those specters of my high school past—and to you, the reader—would be some advice on how to think systematically about questions.

We all want to be consistent, right? I want my movie standards, my dress standards, my choices of hobbies, my political involvement, and my work in the arts and sciences all to cohere in a larger worldview—a larger understanding of how Christians should interact with the culture in which they find themselves. So what I offer here is a bird's-eye view of the larger, overarching questions that will help us be consistent in the way we think. These overarching questions form what we call a *paradigm*.

Paradigm? What's a Paradigm?

A paradigm is "a set of assumptions, concepts, values, and practices that constitutes a way of viewing reality for the community that shares them, esp. in an intellectual discipline."[1] In short, a *paradigm* is a structured way of looking at questions. It answers the big questions, then some specific questions. If you'd like to see a paradigm in skeletal form, flip to pages 102–3. The chart with five views on culture that are labeled, classified, and answer several basic questions is a paradigm. I hope it's user-friendly. This essay will put some muscle on that skeleton. The chart will help *after* you've read the essay.

Did he cook this up himself? you may be asking. Or maybe you're thinking, more accurately, *He's not smart enough to cook this up himself.* Too true. To avoid intellectual plagiarism, I freely admit that I am basically adapting the paradigm offered by H. Richard Niebuhr in his book *Christ and Culture*. Although Niebuhr had some serious theological problems, the paradigmatic work that he does in *Christ and Culture* is just too helpful to pass over. We may *strongly* disagree with a man and still borrow his thought. Where did the Israelites get materials for the tabernacle? On their way out of Egypt— from the Egyptians! It was OK for Israel to use the Egyptians' stuff, but God did not allow Israel to make military alliances with Egypt. Here I'm using Niebuhr's "stuff," but I am *not* allied with Niebuhr.

Since these views are just types, don't take them too rigidly. There's no Christian who holds to one category with complete consistency. Inconsistency within Niebuhr's paradigm is no sin; however, apparently inconsistent approaches to culture should raise red flags and send us to the Bible, for inconsistency with the Bible *is* sin. Anyway, when you read below, understand that I'm giving only an overview. You'll start to see these types all over the place—in people's philosophies, statements, general attitudes, actions, and so forth. When you're discussing issues with someone, you'll know better where to probe to find his underlying assumptions. Now let's look at five views on Christ and culture. (This essay uses the same definition of *culture* as Essay 3.)

Five Views of Christian Response to Culture
Radical Separation

No one can wholly cut himself off from culture, but some people have tried. For example, the early monks, who lived in solitary communities under the law of Christ (they thought), lived as close to absolute separation as they could get. Absolute separation may be impossible in practice, but an attitude of absolute separation is fairly easy to have. Such an attitude is marked by a general suspicion of all things cultural, and it resists any influence from the outside. This view holds that when Christ came to save men, He came to save them *out of* the world; and in so doing, He established something of a totally new culture. Sure, this new culture is on the globe, but in the interests of personal purity, its members remain aloof from world affairs. They have a one-worldly view (one spiritual culture), ignore this earthly world, and seek to live entirely within the terms, values, sensibilities, and traditions of this one spiritual culture.

Radical separationists have a completely negative view of outside culture; to them it is entirely under judgment and dominated by evil. Jehovah's Witnesses have such a view of outside culture; for them, a pledge to the flag is tantamount to siding against Christ. Amish, too, resist the trends of cultural change, living according to a different set of values.

How should we view radical separation? Surely Christianity involves an attitude of forsaking all to follow Christ! No Christian should dispute this. However, to completely abandon the world, to live as if outside of it, is too far (John 17:15; 1 Cor. 5:9–10). There are too many potential false assumptions and consequences involved. One false assumption may be that the source and primary location of sin is somehow in culture. But sin does not work outside in; it works inside out. The monks could run and run, but they could not hide from their own lusts. Likewise, Christians today must remember that no amount of shelter from the world will guarantee freedom from corruption.

Another consequence of totally writing off outside culture is that radical separationists tend to forget that Christ really is in control of *everything*. He created this world, whatever men have done to it. "Though the wrong seems oft so strong, God is the Ruler yet."[2] Furthermore, because radical separationists reject *everything* in culture, they have difficulty dealing with *particular issues* in culture when applying Scripture or refuting error. Why do they have trouble applying Scripture? Answer: the "whole new" culture is too small a context for application. Now, Christ did bring absolute truth (truth that is always true in every situation), but absolute truth is too nebulous and ineffectual without a well-rounded context in which to apply it. The world at large, outside the Christian community, *is* a broad context for application. Ironically, in trying to follow Christ alone, to the exclusion of earthly work, radical separationists trim Christ down from glorious Creator and Ruler of everything to soulwinning leader. If the gospel is only about bringing people into a new culture, then what applications are there for this new (but small) culture? Prayers, Bible reading, and tithing? What do they pray about, and what does the Bible tell them about? The Bible tells us God is loving, but what does God's love mean *out there*?

Radical separationists have trouble not only with the particulars in *application* (as just described) but also in *refutation*. If they automatically condemn everything, why should they even bother studying the nuances of what they condemn? To a radical separationist, even studying such questions is going too far into culture. The problem for the radical separationist is that he can repeat over and over how earthly culture is wrong, but when he actually meets a sin or error in John Q. Smith, he has difficulty recognizing or explaining to John Q. Smith why *that* sin or error is wrong.

Complete Accommodation
If the radical separationists create one spiritual culture, the accommodationists never bother leaving this earthly culture! Let's look at what the accommodationists believe. God put man on the earth. Man is finite, and therefore man has difficulty establishing a good culture in his environment. Finite man's struggle to rise above natural forces leads to conflicts and problems in society too. So man's greatest problem is being small while trying to do big things. But never fear! God is on man's side. God sent Christ into the world to help man overcome his smallness; Christ has come to help each culture fulfill its ideals, whatever the ideals may be.

Are red flags going up for you? I sure hope so. What is missing from this picture? *Sin*! Adam's smallness was no problem in Eden; Eden and Adam were "very good" (Gen. 1:31). When Adam sinned, he morally offended a holy God—a holy God who is the ultimate standard of right and wrong. God cursed the earth, adding *natural* impediments to man's tasks. (Man had been told to have children and subdue the earth; now childbearing and earth subduing hurt.) Man's first problem is moral *sin*, not natural *smallness*. First as a result of sin, and then the curse on sin, come all kinds of other problems. The complete accommodationists reverse that order.

Perhaps you're thinking, *Do Christians really think as complete accommodationists?* Good question, especially since "In Adam's Fall we sinned all" is near the beginning of *The New-England Primer* and is a basic fact of Christianity. I would assert that complete accommodationism, because it has no understanding of *sin*, can have no true understanding of *grace* and *salvation*, either. While members of *Christendom* (a general word for the Christianized world) have held this view, it would be difficult for a true *Christian* to hold it. Perhaps you've heard of the Social Gospel—that is, the view that says that you need to clean up society, remove the taverns, fight poverty, and, *voilà!* you'll make men good because you've bettered their situation. The Social Gospel assumes that Christ came to help us clean up society (a very cultural goal), but it skips over first cleaning up men's hearts.

This view is marked by a general acceptance of all things cultural; God is not the absolute reference point to determine what is wrong, and He has provided Christ to assist any culture to do what it decides is best. This view ultimately reshapes Jesus Christ to be whatever that culture wants Him to be. You can see this today in Liberation Theology and feminist theology: Christ is the great liberator of politically oppressed people groups, the great reformer, the great whatever-you-want-Him-to-be. Christ has been made fluff, and now any goal for the betterment of man is legitimate. Since God and His Word are not the ultimate reference point for ethics, ethics must be based on natural law (laws deduced from observing nature and natural human inclinations), and not God's law.

One must ask proponents of this view, "Why was it necessary for Christ to *die?*" About all they can answer is to be a good example (since they reject the idea of Christ's satisfying God's wrath against man—after all, God is on man's side). But then we must ask, "Is 'a good example' all we need to prevent Muslims from destroying the World Trade Center?" Does Christ assist the terrorists with *their* cultural ideals? Or does He get to be Judge? Furthermore, with such radical and intentional evil in the world, can liberals chalk it all up to natural *smallness?* Hardly.

Combination

Unlike accommodation, this view admits that there is real, moral sin in the world, but this view is not terribly critical of that sin. To this view, this earthly culture is mostly good; but there is so much beyond earthly culture: namely, interaction in the spiritual. Earthly culture is lived in the natural realm, and therefore it's fine for people to live in earthly culture according to natural law. Even non-Christians can get along fairly successfully with natural law; however (and now we're moving into the spiritual culture beyond this earthly one), no one can move toward *super*natural goals without grace. Christ has come to give us grace to be able to rise above culture into the Christian ethic, which is supernatural. Christ adds more. The natural law includes prohibitions of stealing and murder, but the supernatural Christian ethic Christ brought involves principles that can't be deduced from nature, such as turning the other cheek.

Since cultural work is seen as mankind's work that is basically good but not good enough, Christ can take basically good cultural work and use it even in leading men to that good which lies beyond natural man's abilities. Combinationists tend to see the grace of Christ as an add-on, which is a very Roman Catholic conception of grace: God makes up the difference of the little we can offer him. Men can be somehow "good" apart from prior grace. Since cultural work is mostly good, the Christian can participate with his fellow man in cultural endeavors, and then go beyond those cultural endeavors, fulfilling God's purpose for men with the necessary supernatural component. The natural and the supernatural components constitute a two-worldly view of life; the Christian lives in both worlds, using the aspirations in the lower story as stepping stones to the higher.

The biggest problem with this view, which pays only lip service to the sin in mankind's cultural expressions, is that this view's proponents may blindly adopt a wrong cultural pursuit and baptize it with Christ as the fulfillment of that pursuit. Some approaches to the CCM philosophy fall within this view since they begin with the assumption of the basic goodness of all musical genres, not holding musical genres up to criticism as potentially sinful. Since all music is basically good, what it needs to be complete is to have Christ added to it. The problem with this belief is that even musical genres (not just individual songs) are the work of sinful man, and entire genres are potentially tainted. Christianized pop-psychology and the seeker-sensitive church philosophy (which bases ministry decisions on marketing paradigms and what the man in the pew may want) also follow the methodology of coming alongside their audience's desires. They present Christ as the fulfillment of those desires (e.g., peace, personal fulfillment), but they do not critique men's desires thoroughly. What is a lost man's greatest need? Personal fulfillment or reconciliation with an offended God?

Furthermore, since the combinationist view does not *confront* society, it can lapse into the accommodationist view, especially if it is lazy in its talk about sin. Ironically, another problem with the combinationist view is that Christianity may be seen entirely in terms of its cultural garb. How can Christianity be obscured by its cultural trappings? Christ is so often presented as the end-goal of all these earthly desires. But what happens if human desires fluctuate? If people no longer think they need what they used to think they needed, they may not be sure how or why they want Christ any more. Some young people who are "led to Christ" with so many cultural trappings (e.g., "Go to the extreme with Jesus") grow up and then no longer have any tastes for those cultural trappings. They may drift away from Christ altogether. Demographic studies show that this drifting away does happen.

Oscillation

Oscillation means going back and forth; the name for this view implies that the believer's life is lived in a back-and-forth between this-worldly and otherworldly concerns. Perhaps *dualist* is a better term, since it implies life according to *two* principles. This view, unlike the previous two views, reckons with the radical sin in mankind and his culture—defining sin as not just smallness, but offense against God. Nevertheless, unlike the very first view (radical separation), this view understands that earthly culture has its place. Man must live in it, and God can and does work in it. Still, since this culture is so sinful and under God's condemnation, even its best efforts are under condemnation unless done by God's grace. Man's best efforts are filthy rags. Build a church building or build a brothel; apart from God, both acts are sinfully godless.

However, God does work in culture, whether its people acknowledge Him or not. God can work *negatively* in culture, which means that He uses human government with its power of the sword and cultural mores to restrain man from being as evil as he could be. This is a restraint of what is negative more than a proactive construction of a better society. And God can provide for people and show His general love to the world through the work of culture—agriculture, architecture, education, fine arts, government, and so forth.

For believers, God also provides grace in Christ so that they may live with new Christian principles in a fallen world. (This is where the dualism comes in.) The believer now lives a life of faith in God, not offering God his works (cf. Eph. 2:9)—works should be directed toward serving fellow men. Because the believer has faith in Christ, he lives and responds Christianly to what the earthly culture sends his way. God puts believers in places in culture to serve; believers must learn to adapt to their providential locations. So Christians must not withdraw from society but must love their neighbors despite the burdens their culture—whether a totalitarian dictatorship or a hedonistic democracy—places upon them. The essence of such a life is selfless, *agape* living.

Though not my own view, I find this view to be biblically defensible. The great reformer Martin Luther provides a robust example of living godly in the world. Roger Williams, with his views on separation of church and state—radical in his day—is another example of this view. The chief problem for this view is similar to one of the problems of the radical separation view, though to a lesser extent. This view provides little impetus for positive, proactive work in culture (because God works negatively and because Christians are to react rightly where they are). It does not encourage the applying of God's Word to everything. Therefore, it may be less effective in confronting specific sins where they manifest themselves in culture. Furthermore, it seems to create an artificial divide in a believer's activities, even though the Bible seems to indicate that the gospel has far-reaching effects upon every aspect of personality, including the social aspect.

Transformation

I tentatively advocate this final view, though my theological differences with Niebuhr necessitate my advocating it in a different way from his. (Essay 3 offers more explicit parameters with which I agree, though the essay is not necessarily advocating a view.) The transformation view stands side by side with the oscillation view in calling human culture very sinful, but it also recognizes that sin is a blight on a fundamentally good creation of God. God made all things well. God created a being in His image (man) that would procreate and govern (or *cultivate*) a culture over that good creation, but man's sin set God's commanded process askew. Even though the process is askew, the existing culture, though twisted, is not just a necessary evil to keep man from being as bad as he could be. God intended a culture from the start.

Remembering the original creation, the transformationist believes that the new principle of living that Christ brings is not a *completely new* idea, but more of an act of *renewal* of what should have been (Rom. 12:1–2; 2 Cor. 3:18; Col. 3:10). With individual salvation the process of renewing the image of God begins in a man. As this image is transformed in nature, its functions and cultural influences are also transformed (Matt. 28:20). The goal of the believer in culture, then, is to first change the way he does things (to be conformed to God's Word) and then use his work as a confrontation to a sinful society that is going a way God did not intend. By the grace of God and in the power of the Spirit, the Christian will exert his influence and see real changes in people around him.

Conclusion

I doubt I can convey so large a paradigm in so few pages, so I can exhort you only to help me fulfill my modest goal: start thinking biblically. In your discussions, start trying out these questions in the chart (pp. 102–3) and ideas in the essay. See where you agree and disagree with viewpoints on these basic questions and work from there. Survey the Bible for the answers to these questions. Make sure your ideas are consistent, both among themselves and with Scripture (i.e., please don't take my word for it). Ask yourself more questions. For instance, how does a premillennialist's optimism look different from a postmillennialist's optimism? (Premillennialists believe that God's kingdom will not be fully established until the return of Christ. Postmillennialists believe that Christ's return consummates His on-going work of establishing His kingdom through His people.) If you want to be consistent in life, you had much better start with a paradigm—however sparse—than without one.

---

[1]*The American Heritage College Dictionary,* 4th ed., s.v. "Paradigm."
[2]Maltbie D. Babcock, "This Is My Father's World."

	View	Issue		
		What does Niebuhr call this view?	*In how many "cultures" does a believer live?*	*Is the outside culture good or bad?*
Extreme, one-worldly	**Radical separation**	"Christ *against* culture" (a.k.a. "new law")	Entirely in a new, "heavenly" culture brought by Christ	Bad; it must be abandoned.
Extreme, one-worldly	**Complete accommodation**	"Christ *of* culture" (a.k.a. "natural law")	Entirely in this world's culture, which Christ entered	Mostly good; Christ epitomizes cultural ideals.
Moderating, two-worldly	**Combination**	"Christ *above* culture" (a.k.a. "synthetic")	In this present culture, but seeking for a higher culture, often through the best things of this world	Mostly good, but in need of Christ for completion
Moderating, two-worldly	**Oscillation**	"Christ and culture in *paradox*" (a.k.a. "dualist")	In this culture necessarily, also in the new culture, with no close tie twixt the two	Mostly bad; but paradoxically, the believer must learn to live in it.
Moderating, two-worldly	**Transformation**	"Christ *transforming* culture" (a.k.a. "conversionist")	Two; believers attempt to conform the present culture to the ideals of the new culture.	Mostly bad, but Christ changes it for good.

Is there any hope for outside culture?	What is sin's source? How does sin relate to culture?	Do we need a "new" culture? What does "new" mean?	What is history (quoting Niebuhr 194–95) for the Christian?	Who/what may represent this view?
No; get out while you can.	Sin comes from culture itself.	Yes; "new" culture means a wholly other culture to replace this world's culture.	"The story of a rising church or Christian culture and a dying pagan civilization"	Monks in solitary communities; Amish; Jehovah's Witnesses
Yes; all our hopes are earthly hopes.	Sin comes from nature; sin is metaphysical, not moral.	No; we need only to live up to the ideals within present culture.	"The story of the spirit's encounter with nature"	Social Gospel; theological Liberalism; R. W. Emerson
Yes; there are many good things in culture that can point to Christ.	Fallen man's will (also seen in culture, but not reckoned with very seriously here)	Yes; we would be missing the best things in life if we miss the "new" things Christ brought.	"A period of preparation under law, reason, gospel, and church for an ultimate communion of the soul with God"	CCM philosophy; Roman Catholic philosophy (à la Thomas Aquinas)
Not much; God's work in outside culture is mostly preventing further evil.	Fallen man's will (also seen in culture, reckoned with very seriously here, almost pessimistically)	Yes; the "new" culture stands beside the old; believers must relate to both.	"The time of struggle between faith and unbelief, a period between the giving of the promise of life and its fulfillment"	Some of Fundamentalism; classic Lutheranism; Roger Williams
Yes; God has the power to redeem the bad and change it into something good.	Fallen man's will (also seen in culture, reckoned with seriously yet optimistically here)	Yes; Christ's work can make a "new" culture by reforming the old one.	"The story of God's mighty deeds and of man's responses to them"	Some of Fundamentalism; Puritans

Material adapted from *Christ and Culture* by H. Richard Niebuhr.

BEYOND CONTENT ISSUES

by Michael Osborne

Have you ever heard someone say, "The Internet is just a tool; it all depends on what you look at that makes it good or bad"? Hmm. Thinking biblically, are we allowed to stop our evaluation at this simple statement? In light of what the previous essays have said, the above statement is only partly true. *There is more to the Internet than its content: Christians must evaluate the Internet's form as well.* Of course, the Internet harbors both helpful and harmful sites. People can research the gross domestic product of Burundi or destroy themselves with pornography; find an out-of-print classic or lose themselves in a satanic role-playing game. Options such as these should be no-brainers for Bible-believers. But the Internet affects its users in subtler ways than its images. These effects come not from the Internet's content but from *the nature of the Internet itself.* Essay 3 exhorted you in one section to "learn to discern." It looked at direct statements, subtle comments, lifestyle issues, and the fine arts. Now, let's take our Christian discernment up a few notches to examine these potentially insidious effects of the nature of technology itself.

Evaluating Higher-Level Questions

Scripture commands believers to "prove [test] all things; hold fast [tightly] that which is good" (1 Thess. 5:21). We are also commanded, "Ponder the path of thy feet, and let all thy ways be established" (Prov. 4:26). Prudent obedience of the 1 Corinthians 10:31 command to glorify God in all things cannot afford to ignore *anything.* Augustine said, "Prudence is love discriminating rightly between those things which aid it in reaching God and those things which might hinder it."[1] So we will consider as broad a range of questions as we can. First, we'll consider *what* the Internet is and what it does. Next, we'll also ask some deeper questions about motivations in life—the *why* of things—and provide a framework for why we may or may not want the Internet. Finally, we'll examine *how* the Internet works (in light of what it is and does), and how it helps us and hinders us to accomplish good goals.

Evaluating the "What" of the Internet

The first part of this essay's opening statement, "The Internet is just a tool," is true, though the word *just* may wrongly minimize the importance of tools. You've probably heard of Karl Marx, a philosopher who emphasized the "means of production" (i.e., tools) in shaping world history. (Of course, Marx had problems. He figures into this essay only as proof that tools are no small item in a worldview and that if a Christian is to answer Marx, he'll probably have to think about tools too.) A tool helps us accomplish tasks, and the Internet certainly does that. The Internet is a part of *technology*, both in the narrow everyday sense of electronic gizmos and in the broader sense, "the body of knowledge available to a society that is of use in fashioning implements, practicing manual arts and skills, and extracting or collecting materials."[2]

The Bible has something to say about tools. Even idols are tools of a sort. Really. (Read Isa. 44:9–20.) Pagans fashioned gods they regarded as good-luck charms. The gods were *means* to the pagans' *ends*. It may seem ludicrous that a man would labor to fashion a block of wood and then worship that block of wood. But he did, and some men still do. Such is the degrading nature of sin, that man will bow to what is below him to something that he himself made. Instead of using the work of his hands to serve God and man, he makes a god to serve himself.

If the primitive idol technology is obsolete in America, a more "civilized" item of idolatry remains. Even Solomon and Jesus warned about this particular tool/idol—an item not typically seen as a tool, but nevertheless a tool. It yields not mechanical power but economic power. That tool is money (Prov. 11:28; Mark 10:25). Cash, check, plastic, electronic—whatever *physical* form money takes, it is the product of man. Unlike blocks of wood, this tool actually *does* things when we use it. But we must remember money is just an invented tool of man to expedite commerce. A rich man who ignores the fact that all of money's economic power derives from the God who owns the cattle on a thousand hills may rely on sheer economic power to his own damnation (cf. Ps. 50:10; Matt. 6:24). Keeping tools in their proper place is *important*.

Evaluating the "Why" of the Internet

If you read Essay 3, you know that one of the marks of culture is that it is values driven. Individuals and groups holding a range of values want those values embraced by society. The Christian must learn to interact with the world on the level of the "why" (values), and he can do this by recognizing that every "what" (such as the Internet or tools in general) reflects a "why" (cf. Matt. 7:20 principle). This is a *teleological* perspective, meaning a perspective that looks at the *telos*, the end or goal. God had a goal in mind when He willed to create, and so do men, His image-bearers (Eph. 1:10; Rev. 4:11). In a fallen world, men aim at good goals and bad goals, good goals and better goals.

To illustrate seeing the "why" in the "what": what kind of values does a microwave oven reflect? A window shade? An answering machine? A pair of jeans? A chalkboard with chalk and erasers? Here are one or two suggestions per item (respectively): speed in cooking; privacy; control over when and how we communicate; comfortability and durability; and re-usability and visibility. But each of those technologies above represents not just one or two "whys" apiece; rather, each is the result of many generations of cultural dialoguing and debating about values and goals and strategies to meet those goals.

The more a tool is used, the more it fades into the background, taken for granted. But the things we take for granted are the things we take without reference to the God who made them possible and the culture that fashioned them. That is why the rich men in Jesus' encounters and parables had so much trouble: they took money as a matter of course and relied on it (Luke 12:16–21). Have you ever heard about a spoiled child who grew up and wound up in lots of debt? This is because the spoiled child is at risk to see money as something that takes care of him (an idol), rather than something he must take care of and steward things with (a tool). This is a symptom of the Fall, when we forget that God—and not our tools—takes care of us.

Now the only true, right, and workable "why" for the Christian is God's glory and man's good (Matt. 22:36–40; 1 Cor. 10:31). Doing something "for God's glory" can easily become a touchy-feely but contentless dream. Does doing something for God's glory mean simply that I do it with a smile and a fuzzy feeling in my heart? We must make "for the glory of God" *mean* something that we can put into words. One way of doing that is to take all the smaller "whys" (the values) in our lives and make sure they point toward the bigger "whys" (God's glory and man's good). Then, we must learn how to put all the "whats" (the items) under our "whys" (our values). If the Christian is going to take every thought captive for Christ, he will seek to understand the relationships among ideas and ensure that all his ideas are rightly related around Christ and His Kingdom (2 Cor. 10:4–6).

So for the Christian, tools are the work of man's hands. They help him do the work God gave him to do (Gen. 1:26–28). This work is good, and man is justified in trying to do it better. But man must be careful to get his direction and strength from God, not relying on himself or the work of his own hands.

If you're still with me, you may be thinking, "But he's not proved his point. If all these tools can reflect wholesome values, then it comes down to the simple issue of what one does with them." Ah, but have patience. We're still on the runway. Let's take a moment to glance back before we get off the ground.

1. Tools are a significant part of life and important to "get right" in a worldview.

2. Tools, like anything, are significant in part because of the many and varied values they reflect.

3. Christians must arrange their values—and the items that reflect those values—to the glory of God. Fallen man can easily switch his perspective, letting his tools take care of him, shaping his thinking and expectations.

Evaluating the "How" of the Internet

Now *any* of those values that a tool reflects can come back to affect a man's thinking and expectations and even his way of life. Think Nebuchadnezzar (Dan. 4); all the accomplishments of his kingdom led him to think he was really great.

A few preliminary considerations: first, tools' effects on the way we think and act are sometimes subtle. Second, tools are limited in achieving goals. Sometimes tools are so limited in achieving goals that they sacrifice other goals to the ones they are trying to achieve. (For instance, if you write notes to yourself all over the place on little yellow sticky tabs, you have the convenience of being able to stick them anywhere you need to, but you can't collect and organize them all easily.) Tools imply that some goals are more valuable than others. So, we must evaluate *how* tools work and see where they come up short and what they communicate about the priorities of values. Then, we need to evaluate whether the tool's priority of values matches our values.

To illustrate, take gun control—a term with the potential for heated argument in almost any region of the United States. You've seen the bumper stickers: "Fight crime. Shoot back." The one I am particularly interested in here goes, "Guns don't kill people. People kill people." Guns are neither necessary for killing (Cain managed murder without much technology at all) nor necessarily murder machines. But we must admit that guns are mighty useful for killing. A responsible adult acknowledges his shotgun's danger, and whatever his intent for it may be—hunting pheasant, shooting skeet, or defending his home—he cannot leave it out for his five-year-old to play with.

Whatever your position on gun control, the whole fact that there *is* debate underscores the conflict and priorities of values, intended and unintended consequences of owning tools, and how to responsibly handle them. The gun-control issue arrests attention because there is a body count attached to it. When people die, people pay attention. With the Internet, it's a different story. No one dies when someone buys from an online bookseller. But the Internet can involve a conflict of values and unintended consequences, simply because as a tool it reflects multiple values and can, by constant use, affect the way men think and work.

What follows is a grocery list of considerations. The Internet is a valuable tool for the Christian, but the Internet can affect the Christian by changing his thinking, expectations, and way of doing things in ways that could potentially (and of course, not necessarily) impede the advance of the Kingdom. As with the gun-control issue, an awareness of those potential problems may be enough to prevent their being realized.

First, the Internet reflects the value of speed. Fast finding of things (or data) means more time using them, and so the Internet can be a good thing. What incredible power to find the gross domestic product of Burundi in a matter of a minute! However, being accustomed to having so many things *now*, Internet users risk expecting *everything now*. Think Ahab and his desire for Naboth's vineyard (1 Kings 21:1–16). Have you ever used a slower computer and wondered, "What's taking it so long?" if it took more than a few seconds to return search results? Perhaps you're already on your way to ingrained impatience. Be careful. An irony of the speed of the Internet is the amount of time spent on the Internet. It is *very* easy to get caught up with things—no matter how wholesome—that we never intended to look at, but just happened to catch our eye in the search results. In the end, we lose some time, too, from our original plan. Redeem the time (Eph. 5:16)!

Second, the Internet reflects the value of accessibility of vast *quantities* and varieties of information, goods, and services. However, the ease of accessibility is so stunning that we may forget to consider the *quality* of what we have accessed. Heaven forbid, we may let the Internet *think* for us, assuming that the stunning power of finding information constitutes wisdom. It does not. This applies even to Bible software. Just because I can find every use of the word *agapē* in the New Testament and read over it all does not mean I have really drawn truth out of those passages. "Cut-and-paste" theology risks wrongly dividing the Word of Truth (2 Tim. 2:15). We obtained the nuts and bolts of information without sweat, and we are tempted to just screw them in to our own work, assembly-line style, as if somehow we'll automatically do it right. "Why keep researching?" we wonder. "I've got enough stuff already; never mind whether or not I understand it thoroughly." True Bible study is directing the entirety of your multi-faceted personality to the Truth, which is in the final analysis a Person (John 14:6), not a list of texts. But more on that in a moment. For now, remember: INFO≠THOUGHT.

Moreover, accessibility to such a wide variety of goods and information tends to relativize the goods and information (make them look the same); or worse, it gives an advantage to whatever the search engine returns first. Couple such a wide range of quality with the anonymity of the Internet: you do not know the authority and credentials of a given site's author. Oftentimes, for all you know, you are studying economics from a Neo-Marxist. Or you could (as I do frequently in my line of work) run across a theology website by Pastor Pontificator from Podunk, who will deliver truckloads of unstudied bunk and make it look just as good as (or even better than) a respected seminary's resource page. Some people are *not* reliable. Think Rehoboam and the bad advice he followed (1 Kings 12). Proverbs 18:17 says, "He that is first in his own cause seemeth just; but his neighbour cometh and searcheth him." That is, the first fellow to speak in a debate can look pretty convincing, but it's usually necessary to let the other side speak before making a decision. The first site your search engine retrieves is often not the best.

Third, the Internet values convenience in navigation. Welcome to the world of the hyperlinks. Unfamiliar with a term? Simply click on a hyperlink and find sites that explain that term in more depth. Start researching the Magna Carta and end up learning how popes interacted with English archbishops (or topics further afield). Then back to the Magna Carta. But researching this way has many drawbacks, especially in that it interrupts a linear understanding of a topic. Unskilled meandering does not train us to think through points ABC, to properly subordinate ideas (what is central, what is not so important), to cluster arguments accurately, to balance pros and cons proportionally. Ironically, people often find a book's footnotes to be an inconvenient distraction. With the Internet, sometimes all we do is hyperlink our way through what amounts to a series of footnotes. We are left with bricks and no mortar. Good books, however, encourage us to stick with a thought progression, to see how arguments are built over an extended discourse. For instance, if you read Francis Schaeffer's *The God Who Is There,* whether or not you understand everything, you leave with a cogent understanding of the structure of Schaeffer's thought. In a day when many adults have a twelve-year-old's attention span, we must resist the urge to flit from idea to idea. Not only does the Internet not demand focused attention, but it also—along with the remote control—might foster a "browsing" mode for much of life.

Let's illustrate one of the potential dangers of nonlinear learning with the cinematic technique called *montage.* A montage is a series of short film clips juxtaposed to send a message that is more than the sum of its parts. For instance, imagine a film clip with a woman sitting alone at a dinner table set for two, at night. A very brief cut of a speeding ambulance. Back to the woman, slowly drawing the drapes to look out the window. Next, a scene with crowds gathered on a city sidewalk, flashing red lights illuminating faces. Now the woman deliberately dials the telephone. Now paramedics get a gurney from the ambulance. The filmmaker has communicated a great deal, hasn't he? Whomever that woman is waiting for has been in some kind of accident. The filmmaker knows that people intuit ideas based on associated perceptions. The way perceptions are linked together has a great deal to do with our conclusions. Most movies take advantage of montage; the film medium is ideal for communicating that way.

The Internet is a different story. There is no wily director influencing your thinking; rather, you are at the mercy of whatever you run across randomly. Couple this with the relativity and sheer volume of the Internet, and who knows what fragmented and incomplete picture you'll come away with? Even the order that you view sites in is going to affect the way you understand an issue. One of the marks of postmodernism is the fragmentation of truth, and the Internet fosters just such fragmentary perceptions of the world. Postmodernism says that everyone has an opinion and that everyone should be heard. The issues are an innavigable whirlpool, so why form strong opinions?

But issues *can* be clarified and you *can* come to informed opinions, and you need not let the multitude of opinions paralyze you from studying. You *can* have godly wisdom with hard work and faithful petitioning (Prov. 9:1–10; James 1:5–6). One of the great ironies of my life is that I have read countless Internet essays and debates about Calvinism before having ever read Calvin's *Institutes*. I have struggled to understand the nature of the issues, trying to piece them together from others' perspectives, pro, con, indifferent, good, bad, mediocre. By now I could have read the *Institutes* twice. (I finally started last week.)

Fourth, the Internet reflects the value of economy. Firing off an e-mail is quick, if the other person is there to check it. But economy of input means a devaluation of the product, at least in attitude. We throw away the bit of Whopper we cannot finish, but we ask for a doggie bag at the steakhouse. I have a shoebox under the bed of virtually all the notes my wife has given me—even some on index cards. As I recall, I've not saved one e-mail from her. Not only does the wholesale treatment of information and communication create an ethos of disposability and impermanence, but it also does not encourage high culture and effort. I'm sure you've noticed the rise in flagrant abuse of the rules of spelling and grammar in e-mail. A quick send is somehow leading to a quick write, and a quick read (hopefully not overlooking anything as we rush to read the forty-eight other hasty e-mails in our mailbox), and a quick delete. The forward button is the worst offender because our well-meaning friends can drown us with irrelevant jokes, dumb-criminal anecdotes, Christian hysteria rumors about Madalyn Murray O'Hair, and so forth. E-mail economizes needful communication with one hand but with the other often squanders time with irrelevance.

Last, the Internet reflects the values of privacy and personal customization. But the damning irony is that the more people seek their own custom—personalized—experiences, the more they surrender their personality to cyberspace. The Internet is a tool that can let a man extend his personality in relationships with unknown authors and conversation characters in distant lands; but in the process, he may forget his family in the next room or his shut-in neighbor. Porn addicts want control over their own (over)stimulation, but in the end it enslaves their will. People want personal relationships and find it easy to be someone they're not in cyberspace. But dealing with daily annoyances of their flesh-and-blood colleagues becomes increasingly difficult because they'd rather escape than exercise their true personality.

The Internet, billed to bring people together, may break them apart. Think of the computer geek stereotype. "What's with *his* psyche?" you wonder. Well, God has hardwired us (forgive the metaphor) to interact in bodies, with eye contact, handshakes, and holy kisses (you know what I mean!). He put us in a luscious creation and said, "Enjoy." He appeals to our senses, and our senses reinforce things about reality. The suffering of Christ was as *real* as the unleavened bread between your teeth and the fruit of the vine across your tongue. The computer geek stereotype is out of touch with a lot of that because cyberspace is a vaguely surreal world of effervescent information and abbreviated pseudo-personalities. One cannot impart his own soul through cyber-space (1 Thess. 2:8).

With privacy comes distance. The backyard may afford family privacy, but the front porch lets you meet neighbors (assuming they're not on the Internet). With the personal customization of easily con-trolled bits and bytes comes a surrender of many facets of our per-sonality, particularly the relational aspects. It's hard to communicate emotion in pixels, and so someone invented the emoticon. :) It's also easy to swagger on the Internet, adopting a larger-than-life persona as you cruise around and interact with other custom-made personae. The Internet user may wind up with two personalities, one on the Internet, the other off. He may feel less responsible for the Internet personality because, hey, it's anonymous, and it's easy to flame people we can't see. Real-life interaction requires an awful lot of *tact*, while the Internet doesn't.

Another facet of personality we surrender is our creative bent. God made us to be makers. The Internet's arrival was the bar mitzvah of the consumer culture. The consumer culture exults in taking in what we want, when we want, how we want. On the other hand, the Bible extols loving our neighbors with our creative powers, thinking about what they need, not what we want. More advanced, at-the-push-of-a-button technology creates the impression that it is doing the work for us, rather than that we are doing the work with it. We start looking for more labor-saving devices and techniques, even though we were cre-ated for good labor. We start expecting things to be delivered to us, and we forget to exercise our creativity. Part of the image of God in us does not get as well exercised. And worse, we may forget to serve others because we are so busy letting technology serve us.

One last problem of the impersonal nature of the Internet is that it is *not alive*. No matter how much it simulates reality, no matter how much artificial intelligence men invent, our technology is never alive as we are. Not only is it not alive, but also it is not spiritual—that is, it has no spirit. Unfortunately, when we see parallels between man and machine, we speak metaphorically of both, using the parallels from the other. For instance, class time becomes a matter of saving and retrieving data. One of my Greek teachers instructed me to look at myself in the classroom not as a water pump that whirs and grinds and lifts water to great heights—but only wears out over time. Rather, I should see myself as a great redwood, which thirsts for water, lifts it to great heights, and *grows thereby*. This analogy comes closer to the truth (John 4:7–15).

Final Considerations

I doubt I've persuaded you to take a sledgehammer to your PC, which is fine, since that was never my goal. The point of this essay is to get you to think carefully and biblically. If we look closely, we see first that nothing is neutral—no motive, no small item, no method. Technology is not neutral until it promotes a specific message: it brings inherent messages from the start. Usually, if we are aware of the nature and method of a technology, we can curtail its negative effects.

So go ahead and use the Internet when you need to know the gross domestic product of Burundi, but remember that there are real people living in a real place called Burundi. Go ahead and listen to an MP3 debate between a Christian and a Jehovah's Witness, but go read a Watchtower book alongside a good systematic theology volume and write out your own ideas. When you're done ogling Porsche's website, go help your father change the oil on the Buick. Remember that God will hold *you*, the flesh-and-blood you, accountable for every idle instant message (Matt. 12:36). Above all, seek to relate your resources to the highest value: "Prudence is love making a right distinction between what helps it towards God and what might hinder it."

Further Reading

I couldn't possibly hope to cover these points in any depth. If you want to think more closely about some of the issues raised here, I recommend the books by Groothuis and Postman in the bibliography. I have relied extensively on their thoughts for ideas.

---

[1] Augustine, *The Catholic and Manichaean Ways of Life,* trans. Donald A. Gallagher and Idella J. Gallagher, vol. 56 of *The Fathers of the Church,* ed. Roy Joseph Deferrari (Washington; The Catholic University Press, 1966), bk. 1, chap. 15, paragraph 25.

[2] *The American Heritage College Dictionary,* 4th ed., s.v. "Technology."

STUDY QUESTIONS

These questions provoke thought and further study about Internet-related issues. Some questions send you to the Bible, some to the library, some to the chapters, and some to the essays.

1. Explain why it is just for God to be jealous for our love. (Chapter 1 has help on this.)

2. Explain how Internet viewing can be as idolatrous as bowing down to an idol. (Chapter 1 has help on this.)

3. Explain how a person's Internet misuse could indicate that he is unsaved. (Chapter 1 and Essay 1 have help on this.)

4. The Internet powerfully pulls on those who do not expect it. From what *The Dark Side of the Internet* has presented, compare and contrast the Internet to other temptations. (This question is loosely based on Chapter 2.)

5. Archaeologists have discovered ancient pornographic statues. If pornography has practically always been with us, why has the Internet been such a big deal? (Answer from Chapter 3.) Sin in the "arts" is different for different artistic media: drawing and painting, photography, motion pictures, music, literature, and so forth. For instance, what have the electric guitar and extreme amplification capabilities done for music (distortion of sound)? Pick an invention in the arts media and show how it changed the way art/music/literature/speech was done. (This question is loosely based on Chapter 3.)

6. Study David's life in 1 and 2 Samuel with a focus on his sin with Bathsheba. What events in his life foreshadowed his susceptibility to this sin (e.g., how did his relationships with women measure up to God's law)? What was wrong the day of David's sin? What do the penitential Psalms (32 and 51) say about the time between David's sin and its exposure? How did Nathan handle the sin and its exposure? What was the result? (This question is based on Chapter 4 and Essay 2.)

7. Do you know of any contemporary cases where private sin has been exposed? What were the consequences? Were things ever restored? (Do not share these answers with others.) (This question is loosely based on Chapters 4 and 5.)

8. *The Dark Side of the Internet* recommended several methods of keeping yourself from temptation. Which of these have you and your friends used? Which are most effective? Do you have additional ideas that you would recommend to other people? (This question is loosely based on Chapter 6.)

9. How does the Internet resemble the whole world and its culture? How should Christians respond to culture at large? What is culture, anyway? What responses have Christians had to culture? What direction does the Bible offer about our response to culture? How do we apply what we know about culture to questions about the Internet? (The essays will help.)

10. Why was the Internet first invented? What purpose did it serve? What purposes does it serve today? What other technologies have been invented in one setting and eventually used in another? What should humans, who of course are not omniscient, learn from the unexpected applications some technologies have been discovered to have? What might the shift in Internet applications reflect about our culture? (You're on your own for this one.)

11. The Internet is just a baby technology, and we are still learning how to handle it safely and responsibly. When a society tries to handle new technology responsibly and safely, disagreements arise. Research to see if you can compare and contrast the Internet technology (and how to keep it safe) with these other technologies that caused concern: the automobile, television, the atomic bomb. What questions arose? How did different groups of people (political conservatives, liberals, libertarians, Christians) respond to those questions? (You're on your own for this one.)

ANNOTATED BIBLIOGRAPHY

Berg, Jim. *Changed into His Image: God's Plan for Transforming Your Life*. Greenville, SC: BJU Press, 1999. A sound and comprehensive treatment of the doctrine of sanctification and victory over sin. A study guide, a student edition written for teens, and videos/DVDs are also available.

Eliot, T. S. *Christianity and Culture*. New York: Harcourt Brace & Company, 1976. This work includes two shorter Eliot works: "The Idea of a Christian Society" and "Notes Towards the Definition of Culture." Many Christian scholars have relied on Eliot's thought. Eliot's Anglican beliefs about church and state may be a surprise for many Americans.

Groothuis, Douglas. *The Soul in Cyberspace*. Grand Rapids, MI: Baker Books, 1997. This is a superb book from a thoroughly Christian perspective that brings together the best of many theologians and philosophers on technology. A must read.

Myers, Kenneth A. *All God's Children and Blue Suede Shoes: Christians and Popular Culture*. Wheaton, IL: Crossway, 1989. Just what is "pop" culture, and how should the church deal with it? Myers brings up concerns many Christian young people may not have considered yet. He also does not emphasize some of the concerns that many Christian pastors want to emphasize.

Niebuhr, H. Richard. *Christ and Culture*. New York: Harper & Row, 1951. Expanded fiftieth anniversary ed., San Francisco: HarperSanFrancisco, 2001. This is a book of paradigms on how Christians have approached culture. Whatever your personal take on the book, it is regarded as an essential read for anyone discussing the issues. On the heavy side for high school students.

Postman, Neil. *Amusing Ourselves to Death: Public Discourse in the Age of Show Business*. New York: Viking, 1985. How the culture of entertainment has encroached on even the serious and sacred.

———. *Technopoly: The Surrender of Culture to Technology*. New York: Knopf, 1992. Reprint, New York: Vintage Books, 1993. The late Neil Postman was a conservative but secular writer who warned Americans about the subtle effects of technology on our sensibilities. He saw that technological fragmentation has helped bring about a lazy-thinking postmodernism.

Schaeffer, Francis A. *How Should We Then Live? The Rise and Decline of Western Thought and Culture*. Wheaton, IL: Crossway, 1976. How do worldviews work themselves out in culture? How does a Christian approach culture? This book offers wisdom from a master on a crucial question. You may also want to watch the video series by the same name.

Veith, Gene Edward, Jr., and Christopher L. Stamper. *Christians in a .com World*. Wheaton, IL: Crossway, 2000. Both authors have written for *World* magazine and have great experience in keeping Christians abreast of cultural and technological concerns.

Wilson, Wayne A. *Worldly Amusements: Restoring the Lordship of Christ to Our Entertainment Choices*. Enumclaw, WA: Wine-Press Publishing, 1999. This author sounds a strong warning about Christians who buy into the world's bunk philosophies of entertainment.

Wingren, Gustaf. *Luther on Vocation*. Translated by Carl C. Rasmussen. Philadelphia: Muhlenberg Press, 1957. This book is an excellent explication of the fourth view of Christ and culture, discussed in Essay 4. Whether or not you agree with Lutheran distinctives, this book is a clear demonstration of how theology is applied to day-to-day life. Reprints are available from the Cranach Institute at Concordia University in Wisconsin.

For some helpful links and additional information, visit the BJU Press resources page on the Internet at www.bjup.com/resources/ and navigate through secondary Bible to *The Dark Side of the Internet*.